The Community of States

The Community of States

A Study in International Political Theory

edited by
James Mayall

London
GEORGE ALLEN & UNWIN
Boston   Sydney

© George Allen & Unwin (Publishers) Ltd, 1982
This book is copyright under the Berne Convention. No reproduction
without permission. All rights reserved.

George Allen & Unwin (Publishers) Ltd,
40 Museum Street, London WC1A 1LU, UK

George Allen & Unwin (Publishers) Ltd,
Park Lane, Hemel Hempstead, Herts HP2 4TE, UK

Allen & Unwin, Inc.,
9 Winchester Terrace, Winchester, Mass. 01890, USA

George Allen & Unwin Australia Pty Ltd,
8 Napier Street, North Sydney, NSW 2060, Australia

First published in 1982

British Library Cataloguing in Publication Data

The Community of states.
I. Mayall, James
327   JX1395
ISBN 0-04-320151-2

Library of Congress Cataloging in Publication Data

Main entry under title:

The Community of states.

Includes index.
1. International organization – Addresses, essays, lectures. 2. International
relations – Addresses, essays, lectures. I. Mayall, James
JX1954.C57843 1982   341.2   82-11414
ISBN 0-04-320151-2

Set in 10 on 11 point Plantin by Typesetters (Birmingham) Limited,
and printed in Great Britain
by Billing & Sons Ltd, London and Worcester

Contents

Preface

This is the second production by an inter-university group which first met in 1974 and has continued to meet at regular intervals since to discuss theoretical questions in the study of international relations. The first was *The Reason of States* edited by Michael Donelan (Allen & Unwin, 1978).

We thank the London School of Economics and Political Science for assistance towards the cost of our meetings and the University of Exeter Research Fund Committee which made possible a weekend meeting of the group in the summer of 1979. We are indebted in various ways to many others and particularly to Elizabeth Leslie for her help in the final preparation of the manuscript.

THE AUTHORS

The Authors

Christopher Brewin — *Lecturer in International Relations, the University of Keele*

Peter F. Butler — *Lecturer in Politics, the University of Exeter*

Michael Donelan — *Senior Lecturer in International Relations, the London School of Economics and Political Science*

Zdenek Kavan — *Lecturer in International Relations, the University of Sussex*

James Mayall — *Senior Lecturer in International Relations, the London School of Economics and Political Science*

Cornelia Navari — *Lecturer in Political Science, the University of Birmingham*

Barrie Paskins — *Defence Lecturer in the Ethical Aspects of War, the University of London, King's College*

Alan Pleydell — *Formerly Department of Politics, University of Southampton*

Brian Porter — *Senior Lecturer in International Politics, the University College of Wales, Aberystwyth*

Hidemi Suganami — *Lecturer in International Relations, the University of Keele*

John Vincent — *Lecturer in International Relations, the University of Keele*

Moorhead Wright — *Senior Lecturer in International Politics, the University College of Wales, Aberystwyth*

The Community of States

Introduction

JAMES MAYALL

This book explores the meaning and implications of an idea which is frequently employed in public discussion of world affairs but seldom taken seriously or analysed. The concept of an international or world community is most often invoked for one of two reasons. The first is to characterise, in a convenient shorthand, the present stage of world history. As Czeslaw Milosz put it in his 1980 Nobel Lecture: 'carried forward as we are by the movement of technological change we realise that the unification of our planet is in the making and we attach importance to the notion of international community'.[1] The second reason is to indicate a need for the reorganisation of international relations according to principles of distributive justice.

Although these two reasons are logically distinct they tend to appear together; the fact that the world is integrated in a technological and economic sense is advanced by liberal thinkers as sufficient justification for the development of a new sense of international responsibility. In much the same way an earlier generation of liberal internationalists argued that the destructiveness of modern warfare between nation-states revealed that the state itself was an anachronism and that the time had come to match the worldwide achievements of modern science and technology with world government.[2]

The world did not listen then; it seems unlikely that it will listen now. Nor should this surprise us. What, after all, is this international community on the basis of whose shadowy existence we are supposed to change our current attitudes and behaviour, if not to surrender our political identity? Neither the defenders of a new international morality nor those who claim that global unification is a matter of fact tell us. Nor, with more excuse, do the professional students of international relations. After the utopian moralising of the interwar period their primary objective was to establish the study of international relations as a branch of positive political science, to chart and measure by empirical observation and with the aid of formal logic the world we live in. In other words they mostly avoided philosophical questions as unlikely to yield positive answers.

But if one laudable aspect of positive political science was its realism – no one talks these days as though world government were the logical next step and a mere question of political will – it also left us ill prepared to think seriously about the moral basis of international action in an increasingly integrated world. During the years of unchallenged Western affluence and American supremacy, for many this hardly seemed an important question; indeed it was fashionable to hold that both ideology and political philosophy were dead. In recent years, however, as our political and economic future has become increasingly uncertain there has been a renewed interest in questioning the fundamental basis of our institutions and practices, the beginnings of a debate about the possibility and nature of international political theory to match the global interdependence which has been so exhaustively analysed in the empirical literature.

Like its predecessor, *The Reason of States*, this book has been written as a contribution to this debate. Its two major presuppositions are the same, namely, that international relations cannot properly be studied in isolation from the study of the state itself and that a central element in any international political theory must be an account of the moral bonds between men living in separate states. If, as I have suggested, the appeal to our membership of an international community as a source of international morality lacks credibility, it is because the nature of obligation beyond the frontiers of the state is not, as such appeals generally assume, self-evident. To explore the nature of obligation is to explore the meaning of community, of what it is that men hold in common and why.

From this standpoint several questions suggest themselves. What, if any, are the communitarian assumptions on which foreign policies are based? Is some sense of international community a necessary prerequisite for a world organised according to principles of order and justice? And, if it is a prerequisite, what is its essential character, how may it come about and on what is it to be grounded?

The answers to these questions are also neither self-evident nor are they uncontested. And because this is so there seems little advantage in opening the inquiry with a pre-selected definition of community to test against the reality of international politics. Although several chapters contain definitions, the differences between them are often merely semantic. Behind these surface differences there lies an important substantive question: whether community is to be regarded as in some sense natural, the lost world which we must seek to regain, or, on the contrary, as the end-state in a process of deliberate and rational creation. It is with such substantive questions about the nature, possibilities and limitations of community in international relations that this book as a whole is concerned.

The first task, however, will be to map the terrain, the thought-world within which the inquiry is to take place (Chapter 1). There are traps here. Since the seventeenth century Western political theory, that is, large-scale reflection on the nature and ends of politics, has been predominantly concerned with the justification of authority and the basis of civil society. This preoccupation has notoriously confined the consideration of international relations to the margin of the Western philosophical tradition. It has also bequeathed to international thought a metaphor which is at once powerful and in important respects misleading. International life, we are often told, is like the original state of nature, a state of war ceaseless and unedifying. The metaphor is powerful because it dramatises what is indeed a prominent feature of the landscape, the absence of any central authority and the consequent possibility that states will choose to settle their disputes by recourse to arms rather than to law. But it is misleading because the international arena is not, except in a purely formal sense, like a state of nature at all.

The most obvious respect in which the international arena differs from the state of nature is in respect of history. It is true that the concept itself emerged at a particular point in Western intellectual life, in other words, that it can no more escape its time than any other human idea or artefact. Nevertheless that is, of course, precisely what it tries to do. As an idea, the state of nature is essentialist: it portrays a never changing instinctual world. The contemporary society of states, on the ·other hand, is an historical creation; its members share preoccupations, which is to say memories, that their predecessors did not entertain. To share even a preoccupation is to move out of the state of nature in its essential meaning; it is also to accept that the character of international society will change. For example, over the past 200 years ideas about the nature of the state, considered as a form of human association, have changed radically and so too, as a consequence, have ideas about the nature of the community of states. How are we to account for such a change? What was it, for example, which led Kant to include in his sketch of *Perpetual Peace* only one cosmopolitan right, namely, a universal right to hospitality, whereas the Brandt Commission, whose report was published in 1980, envisaged an international community supported by mechanisms designed to transfer resources from the rich to the poor member countries 'as of right'? Clearly the range of available ideas about the proper role of the democratic state was considerably narrower in 1795 when Kant's pamphlet was published than in 1980. But why?

The answer to such a question can only be historical. No doubt political arguments are few in number and are in principle applicable to any age or place. But the issues on which these arguments are deployed as well as the language in which they are couched and the forces which are enlisted on their behalf inevitably bear the hallmark of the age. Arguments must be weighed on their merits; but it is not their merits, or at least not their merits alone which determine why some issues and not others become the focus of debate at a particular time, nor the passion with which they are pursued. History not philosophy sets the agenda of international politics.

The issues and ideas which dominate the international agenda at the present time in the fields of political, military and economic affairs, emerge clearly from a survey of contemporary international society. They all derive in one way or another from that condition of the modern world which, as I have already noted, is often described as interdependence. More particularly they derive from one aspect of that condition: the fact that, as the world has been integrated militarily – in that the rivalry of nuclear powers knows no geographical limits, economically – in that all five continents are now involved in a global division of labour, and intellectually – in that, as De Tocqueville prophesied, industrial society with its egalitarian values has established itself as the universal model, the state has everywhere extended its prerogatives and entrenched its power. It has not withered away in the socialist East, as Marx had predicted, nor been willed away in the West as the liberal internationalists had hoped. In the Third World, politics is about establishing the state, competing to control its apparatus and to administer its patronage; the idea of transcending or going beyond the state would seem to most Third World politicians a ludicrous fantasy. Nowhere indeed is it a serious issue.

The modern world is thus still a world of states, but states which are forced to coexist in a more uncomfortable intimacy than ever before. It is this unprecedented intimacy which gives contemporary international relations their distinctive character and gives to the question of external obligation a special prominence. When diplomacy takes place in the knowledge that the great powers possess a destructive potential unparalleled in human history; when the increased scale of economic interaction and the spread of literacy and modern education are as likely to increase as to reduce the scope for conflict between peoples; when no more than in the past will any government willingly surrender power but when, unlike the past, all *claim* to speak in the name of *The People*, what arrangements are possible for the common good? What in short is to count as right action in foreign policy?

No answer to this question can be attempted without subjecting the state and its customary justification to some further analysis (Chapter 2). If this seems a conventional approach it is also a necessary one. The tendency in much recent writing on international politics to look at relations (and systems of relations) rather than entities was useful in exposing the fiction of the potentially autarkic, literally independent, state (that is, one freed from causation); but it is a useless vantage-point if we wish to secure purchase on the moral problems of international life for the simple reason that morality assumes accountability and one cannot hold a system of relations accountable for anything. If both statesman and citizen can be held accountable it is because they are assumed to have identities which persist over time: whatever their causal status, therefore, as moral agents they are free.

The fact that we view politics in this way, and that we can only make sense of the political world as an arena of moral choice, perhaps explains one of the seeming paradoxes of the modern world, namely, the triumph of the doctrine of legal sovereignty at precisely the time that the world is widely perceived as more interdependent and governments more constrained, more caught up in a web of systemic causes beyond their control, than ever before. This statement may itself seem paradoxical, but reflection will, I believe, show that it is not so; the possession of sovereignty is often thought of as conferring immunity from moral constraint; but its essence is the assertion of freedom without which there can be no morality. Unless one is free to choose, one's choices cannot sensibly be evaluated. There are, of course, historical reasons which also help to explain the triumph of the doctrine of sovereignty: between the seventeenth and twentieth centuries it had great appeal for political societies undergoing radical transformation and in need of a new justification of authority. But justification and judgement are two sides of the same coin: only free states can be held up for judgement.

How they are to be judged is a different matter. It will depend very largely on whether the sovereign states are seen as the final source of moral authority, as Hobbes maintained, or whether, on the contrary, the exercise of sovereign authority is itself subject to a moral law which exists independently of, or at least beyond, the state. Over the centuries this moral law has been variously represented as deriving from a wider contract between states, from the rational self-determining individual and from a natural order which binds all men in a single worldwide community. I shall return to these alternative positions shortly; the point to note here is that while the doctrine of sovereignty establishes the freedom, and therefore the moral accountability of the state, it does not assume that the decisions of the sovereign are necessary moral.

The development of the doctrine of sovereignty from a theory of dynastic to a theory of popular right after the French Revolution, and the linking of the doctrine to nationalist ideology from the mid-nineteenth century onwards, undoubtedly weakened the appeal to a superior moral law, whether divine, contractual, or individualist (Chapter 3). The nationalist argument stipulates that every man has a nationality as part of his essential being, that the basis of the community, in other words, is not only national but natural, and that the political order should therefore correspond to this natural and national order. Clearly such an ideology raises problems about any wider community. In principle the problems are not insurmountable:

so long as nationality can be empirically and unambiguously determined and the political map drawn accordingly, why should a nationalist world not also be an harmonious one? In practice nationality is neither natural nor unambiguous and the doctrine that the nation exhausts the moral space within which men live, whatever its undoubted sociological, psychological and historical appeal, sets severe limits on any wider international community.

There is a further difficulty. The doctrine of sovereignty asserts the freedom and therefore entails the moral accountability of the state; but nationalist ideology asserts that this accountability should be to the national group itself. 'My country right or wrong' neatly summarises both the appeal of the conventional position (for in the last resort I cannot be expected to surrender my natural identity and loyalty) and also its failure to establish an unimpeachable source of right (for in such a self-referring world how could one establish what was wrong?). It seems that the two major supports of the contemporary international order pull in opposite directions – towards a principle of moral accountability on the one hand and towards moral scepticism on the other.

Fortunately the position is not quite as serious as this summary suggests. The necessity of coexistence has, in practice, modified the solipsism of the nation-state, while the conventions of diplomacy, international law and international business have provided a broad set of standards by which foreign policy can be evaluated. The task of working out these practical principles in the absence of any authoritative external moral law has fallen to the lawyers, economists and those practitioners of state-craft, who have traditionally regarded foreign policy as an autonomous field of action. Whether or not their 'operational philosophies' already rest on communitarian assumptions, a claim which most positive international lawyers and realists would no doubt deny, or can be developed in a way which will help to create a genuine international community in response to the alleged imperative of interdependence, is a matter which we debate in four chapters of this book.

A development of this latter kind – that is, the emergence of an international community the rules of which would be voluntarily accepted by *all* member states in the interests of justice and order – would have to meet two conditions. First, if it were to be a binding legal community between sovereign states, its rules would have to be based on the principle of reciprocity. No doubt there could be agreed exemptions from some of the economic although not the political obligations of membership (as there are already in some international economic programmes which include provisions to favour the poorest states), but the principle of reciprocity itself could hardly be surrendered without the creation of supranational authority (Chapter

4). Second, since the primacy of state interests has always been held by the practitioners of *Realpolitik* to place foreign policy ultimately above the law, although not of course beyond constraints imposed by prudence, any such community would have to reflect the emergence of a widely held perception amongst governments that common interests not only exist but in the contemporary world are synonymous with state interests (Chapter 5).

The most obvious test of this thesis arises from the existence and deployment of nuclear weapons (Chapter 6). Time and again in human history men have failed to unite in the name of the greater good, a concept so elevated that it could always be interpreted according to taste and interest. But the great powers now possess weapons which are effectively capable of destroying life on earth. The question which this terrifying prospect prompts is whether the *summum malum* may yet convince the most realistic of statesmen of the need to create a wider community of interest where appeals to the *summum bonum* have traditionally failed. If the strategic doctrines of the two superpowers provide ample ground for doubt, their attempts to control the testing of nuclear weapons and the negotiation of the Non-Proliferation Treaty, precarious and contentious as these achievements are, at least provide us with room for hope. The best that can be said, perhaps, is that mercifully the thesis has not been put to the final test.

The integration of world markets is also often urged as the ground on which it may be possible to construct an international community of interest (Chapter 7). In this case too the evidence is equivocal. It is true that of the practical thinkers whose ideas about community we consider, the liberal economists have come closest to adopting this view. One reason may be that while their profession has benefited from the rise of the modern nation-state, they have never felt at home with it intellectually. Economists have benefited from the state because, as it has extended its prerogatives and assumed new responsibilities, governments have looked to them for professional and theoretical guidance. Their unease, on the other hand, arises because their central aim has been to discover causal behavioural laws not moral ones. From the start, therefore, economists have anchored their theories in a view of human nature as rational and self-interested which is at once individualist and universal. The state is the contingent setting within which they happen to work, but not more than that. In practice, of course, economists have not been slow to use their professional expertise in the service of this or that moral cause, that is, to advocate policies on the grounds that they would have beneficial consequences. But the difficulties they face in immunising the allegedly positive laws of economics from disputes about justice, for example in the North–South debate, inevitably calls in question the proposition that the community, whether national or international, can be grounded solely on rational self-interest. Interest may indeed be necessary for any community to exist but it is clearly not sufficient.

The limitations of a view of community which rests solely on interests are the limitations of the conventional morality of states. If this position cannot yield satisfactory criteria on which international obligations can be based and against which foreign policy can be held up for judgement what alternatives are available? We consider two here. The first is based on the view, which we owe to Kant, that the individual is not only the major obstacle to human improvement because of his constant surrender to base passion but also, through the development of his moral reason, the only possible agent of progress (Chapter 8). On this view it is the faculty of moral reason which provides us with two independent criteria for use in evaluating foreign policy, namely, that action should always be based on a maxim which is capable of translation into an universal law, and that similarly the individual should under all circumstances be treated as an end in himself and never merely as a means.

In theoretical studies of international relations, Kant has sometimes been represented as a revolutionary or utopian thinker; it is important to recall, therefore, that he was not particularly optimistic about the rate at which the 'liberation' of humanity through rational morality could be achieved. His purpose was rather to show what conditions would have to be met if it was to be achieved. One of the difficulties which follow from the nature of this project is that the criteria listed above, so precise and clear in outline, are not much help in judging hard cases. How, for example, is one to judge action which, while clearly not in conformity with international right under the two criteria, can be said none the less to be moving in the right direction?

There is also a problem of translating the Kantian argument to fit the circumstances of the contemporary interdependent world. His view of the international community is so minimalist, confined in fact to a confederation of states pledged to non-aggression, that it is difficult to know how he would have viewed contemporary efforts to prescribe universal norms of economic and social behaviour or the tendency to make the propagation of fundamental human rights an object of foreign policy (Chapter 9). The assertion that such rights exist, and their codification in the Universal Declaration, may, however, reasonably be taken as evidence that governments accept in principle the proposition that men share a common humanity and must be treated as ends in themselves, even if their disputes over how these human rights are to be interpreted and protected show how far short of the Kantian community we still fall.

The second, although older, alternative to the conventional position is to ground our obligations to others, including to those who live in other political societies, in a natural law under which mankind as a whole constitutes a natural community (Chapter 10). On this view man is not only naturally social but equally has a natural bias to the good. Foreign policy is not, therefore, and has never been inspired by altruism, let alone by mere self-interest but by 'interest considered right'. The idiom in which this original morality is expressed changes with the times but not the natural necessity, it seems, to incline to the right. Thus where nineteenth-century European statesmen were much concerned with honour, their modern equivalents speak of responsibility; both, however, are as concerned with their position within a wider moral community as they are with the pursuit of self-interest.

Natural law has been a minority position in Western intellectual life since the decline of religion; indeed for many its theological associations probably disqualify it from serious consideration. Yet, before it is summarily dismissed as anachronistic by those in search of a purely secular scheme of values, it is worth reflecting how deeply rooted is our conception of good, and of its priority over evil – no one speaks, for example, of protectng their illegitimate interests. Those who as citizens perpetuate evil acts are generally thought of as pathological, as are political leaders who quite deliberately and with sadistic pleasure oppress the populations over whom they rule or wilfully destroy other nations. It is not difficult in the history of the twentieth century to think of examples.

If, as the philosophy of natural law teaches, our natural bias is not solely towards the pursuit of private interest which must then be restrained externally but towards the pursuit of interest considered right, then it is not merely our leaders who must be judged by the standards of honourable or responsible behaviour but all of us: we are all members of the community of mankind. The problem here is one of scale. The great issues of the day, the preservation of peace, global recession, the world population and food crises, and so on, all demand action; but because they are so awesome they do not translate easily into the language of individual obligation. In what sense can we all be held responsible for the solution of these problems? One possible procedure for translating the requirements of natural law into a practical ethic of responsibility is to consider what is involved in behaving responsibly in the private and public roles which we occupy (Chapter 11). In this way perhaps the community of mankind whose existence, as I suggested at the outset, is so often invoked without explanation or analysis can be realised piece by piece.

Having surveyed the limitations of the conventional morality of states and discussed some alternatives, it could be argued that our inquiry should end at this point. We conclude, however, with a challenge to both the conventional position and the alternatives (Chapter 12). If the claim that there is a moral community of mankind is less easily dismissed even by those sceptical of natural law than in the past, it is presumably because cultural differences no longer divide societies and governments as deeply as once they did. There are stronger forces at work, in effect coercing them to coexist within a common social and diplomatic world. In part these forces are economic but, in so far as states generally are concerned to establish their legitimacy within the international community, they are ideological (cf. Chapter 1). Thus language and idiom are necessarily involved in any discussion of international legitimacy. Once it was Christian civilisation which provided the cultural and symbolic framework for the Western Society of States; in the contemporary world it is the common preoccupation of states with the organisation of material life. The appeal for economic co-operation, as Martin Wight was perhaps the first student of international relations to perceive, now occupies a parallel place in international diplomacy to the invocation of Christendom against the Turk in Western diplomacy before 1856.[3]

But how deep does this new language go and at what cost is it being imposed? Most of the authors in this book assume that, while the international environment may have changed, the identity of states and citizens remains much as it always was. Indeed I have suggested that this is a necessary assumption if men are to be regarded as moral agents and hence held accountable for their actions. But there has been an alternative view available in Western thought at least since the nationalist reaction to the European Enlightenment. On this view, the integration of the world and the visions of 'modernity' which now inspire men everywhere are systematically destroying those natural historic cultures, which are the necessary support of our identity and hence also of our capacity for moral action. As Herder put it: 'the savage who loves himself, his wife and his child . . . and works for the good of his tribe as for his own . . . is . . . more genuine than that human ghost, the . . . citizen of the world, who, burning with love for all his fellow ghosts loves a chimera. The savage in his heart has room for any stranger . . . the saturated heart of the idle cosmopolitan is a home for no-one.'[4]

The power of this challenge should not be underestimated. A craving for collective as well as individual authenticity, for what belongs to us alone and not to mankind, is as much a part of the modern mind as the opposite craving for universal modernism. But it should not be thought that this view disposes of the need to think about international community: on the contrary, to the extent that it is accepted, the need becomes more urgent. The enforced intimacy of the modern world is a brute fact; romantic savagery is not an option. In the version of the challenge presented here, an attempt is made to reconcile the romantic and classical traditions within Western thought. It is argued that we need to distinguish more sharply than at present between culture and community on the grounds that, while cultural diversity remains a necessary support for our identity, the development of community depends on formal and legal principles, on our capacity to join together not to merge our separate identities but to preserve them. More than ever before we need to conceive of an international community which can transcend cultural boundaries without destroying them.

NOTES: INTRODUCTION

1 Printed in the *New York Review of Books*, 5 March 1981.
2 The literature on the need for world government is extensive and all but forgotten. Two examples, celebrated in their day and retrieved from a second-hand bookshop almost at random, are Henry Noel Brailsford, *Olives of Endless Age* (New York: Harper, 1928) and Emery Reeves, *The Anatomy of Peace* (Harmondsworth: Penguin, 1947).
3 Martin Wight, *Power Politics* (Harmondsworth: Penguin, 1979), p. 302.
4 Herder, *Ideas for a Philosophy of the History of Mankind*, quoted in Isaiah Berlin, *Vico and Herder, Two Studies in the History of Ideas* (London: Hogarth Press, 1976), p. 178.

Part One
The Contemporary Order

1
Diplomatic Structure and Idiom

CORNELIA NAVARI

The society of states is often characterised as an anarchical society, there being no elaborated constitutional order which sets the terms of disputes and establishes rules for the relations of the combatants. Others would claim that it is an ideological vacuum where power alone rules. Indeed, there are some who would not characterise it as a society at all but rather as a State of Nature. But, in fact, the difference between these characterisations is minimal; to Hobbes, from whom we derive the modern usage, the State of Nature was such because there existed in it no laws, rules, or common understandings.

Yet, despite these characterisations, it is a fact of historical record that statesmen have aspired to create regularised, if not legalised, practices for the mutual regulation of their relations. The rules of diplomatic exchange were laid down very early. They were followed by rules on neutrality, on extra-territoriality, on jurisdiction, on war itself.

Not only do rules exist, but both the rules and the modes of producing them have shown an unsteady, but definite, historical tendency to increasing elaboration, specificity and discrimination. In the early eighteenth century, the only generally agreed practices upon which a statesman would have relied with any certainty were the limited body of rules concerning ambassadorial representation; for commercial practices or the treatment of foreign nationals, he would have had to consult a particular treaty worked in the recent past between his government and one or two others. Today, numerous international organisations are producing extensive rule sheets of general application.

Behind these legal structures, inspiring them, have been generally accepted idioms of debate, common political forms and ways of perceiving the world. Thus, we can speak about the diplomacy of the Ancien Régime in general, with its concern for marriage contract and war, alongside the particular diplomacies of eighteenth-century England or France. Furthermore, we can distinguish that diplomacy from the 'new' diplomacy of the modern nation-state, with its concern for parliamentary forms and war-avoidance, without speaking nonsense.

The form of these structures reflects the predominant form of the state at any given time and the current ideas of political order that produced it. Thus, the diplomacy of the Ancien Régime mirrored externally the internal state organisation of the Ancien Régime and its regulating political theories. Its diplomacy of marriage and war mirrored its notions of the role of the Royal House and inheritance rights, while the sacred egotism of its separate monarchical houses towards one another was paralleled by the self-same egotism at home. The cabinet government of the nineteenth century was paralleled by the *Europäisches Kabinett* – meetings in cabinet form of Europe's leading ministers. The present democratic order of the state system is a reflection of the democratic state with its intermittent demands for strong direction and its extensive bureaucratic structures.

This peculiar parallelism derives from the undoubted fact that the state serves itself and that statesmen in their relations with one another evolve structures appropriate to their evolving states. Hence it was that, as Britain industrialised and its emergent industrial economy came to depend on high mobility of the factors of production, it passed from ensuring such mobility at home to creating it abroad. In this sense, the Anglo-French Treaty of Commerce served the same general ends as Poor Law Reform. In the degree to which other European states began to industrialise, they began to experience some of the same needs. In consequence, the demand for more freedom of movement became a general demand and a structure of more open trade gradually emerged.

But each state does not have a separate and distinct 'mind' which anticipates its own needs. Its needs are rather the product of human thought and example – the thought of an Adam Smith or the example of an efficient and unified France – thoughts and examples, moreover, which are seldom contained within the tidy legal structures of territorial boundaries. The thoughts, examples and experiences which formed Germany, Turkey and Iraq derived from sources which lay outside the territory in question, sources which provided inspiration to those within and patterns for state-building.[1] How else can we explain the fact that dynastic *states* were succeeded by liberal *states*, by nationalist *states*, by modernising *states*? 'Stateness' itself would not exist but for some general agreement that, as a political form, the state is a good thing.

The general spread of common ideas of political legitimacy and the development of similar political structures is encouraged, not impeded (as is often thought), by the existence of a state system. The condition of sovereign bodies and the looseness of any overarching legal structures makes 'being unlike' either a threat or a weakness and encourages political leaders to imitate the features of the strongest, so far as they are able. 'If citizens fight like that', Frederick William III is reported to have said after the disastrous battle at Jena, 'then all Prussians must become citizens.'[2]

The fact that ideas of legitimacy and patterns of state-building move across territorial boundaries was explored by Martin Wight in an essay, first published in 1972, entitled 'International Legitimacy'.[3] In it, he detected, and deplored, a growing tendency for Revolution to be considered a justifiable method for accomplishing political change. The tendency was well observed. It is, indeed, one of today's 'common understandings' and one whose emergence has perplexed many liberal thinkers. Less clear were his reasons for referring to this phenomenon as 'international' legitimacy, as if there were two sorts, one operating abroad and the other at home. The ideas of legitimacy which were making Revolution more legitimate abroad were the same ideas which were justifying it at home.

The fact that the same political referents may orient politicians and revolutionary leaders and citizens in different states, may lead to the adoption of similar state forms and certainly accounts for the rise of a common diplomatic language: none of this ought to be taken to mean that political ideology is not also disputed between states, quite obviously. Nor is it to deny that the same words may mean different things to different people, or that some may even use the words signifying legitimacy for their own gain and mean nothing at all by them. Not all Divine Right monarchs actually believed that God spoke to them, just as we may doubt that all Third World statesmen are really committed to development. What it does mean is that the society of states is not without a body of shared and disputed values, ideological obsessions, or requirements for hypocrisy, and that some may, at times, prevail over others.

It is because there are similar political forms, or the aspiration to create them, emerging out of similar political goals and giving rise to agreed rules, that we can speak of a society of states. It is these common political forms, similar ideological objectives and resultant legal structures that constitute the society, give it its texture and form. Indeed, the description of the society of states is nothing other than the description of its prevailing state forms, its prevailing idiom of values and its prevailing legal structures, through particular historical periods.

Its historical specificity is a condition which perhaps ought to be stressed. If rulers have everywhere been prepared to be hypocritical, the language of their hypocrisy has changed. If everywhere they have promised what they cannot deliver, what they have promised has changed. The society of states, like any society which changes, is an historically specific society. It is the creation of historically specific legal structures and historically specific common understandings.

The prevailing notion of the proper ends of political order which pervades the contemporary society of states is a creation of nineteenth-century social theory. Its distinguishing legal structures were created after the Second World War.

CONTEMPORARY NOTIONS OF POLITICAL LEGITIMACY

The starting-point for most contemporary political myths lies in a particular view of man, a view which makes him highly dependent on society's arrangements. In the modern thought, men are not simply creations of nature. While having, in fact, the same natural attributes, they are considered to be formed and placed by social arrangements. For a person to become fully human, society must be of a certain nature. The purpose of the state is to bring society into that condition.

The emphasis on social movement in current ideological postures carries with it other correlative ideas; change, transformation and in particular the notion of transition have all become extremely important in the contemporary idiom. Hence, also, the considerable attention paid today to transitional societies, societies which are moving from some general notion of 'traditional' to another general notion of 'modern'. Such societies present a grand spectacle of the progress, with all its attendant accidents, that all men must go through to realise their collective and, eventually, individual potential.

Man may be proletarian, or Serbian, or black, but in most current myths he shares one common characteristic. He is found everywhere in a condition of inequality, whereas it is in his basic nature to be equal. The achievement of equality is the basic value to which most contemporary societies pretend, whatever the obvious differences among current political mythologies, and most states are judged by their ability to achieve equality among their citizens.

Equality is not the only god which modern society serves. There is also Efficiency – the rational use of man's energies – which coexists with equality particularly in more advanced societies and coexists with it in a kind of tension. In more traditional societies, the drive for equality coexists with older religious or social ethics involving gross inequalities, often, too, in considerable tension. Different societies break at different points in their social compromises.

But crusades on behalf of efficiency alone would scarcely justify the state machine of a developed country. Rather, efficiency must also be seen to be promoting the well-being of a large mass of the people and often it is an integral part of the equality drive itself. Similarly, those who use traditional tribal language in underdeveloped countries often do so as the representatives of groups who feel themselves disadvantaged in the scramble for the goods of society at large and who wish more equal shares of those goods.

So deeply held is the belief in, and the commitment to, equality, that even where their social circumstances are not in fact rapidly equalising, men are still deemed capable of visualising themselves in ways quite at variance with those circumstances. Even peasants, thanks to Mao, can now make revolutions.

The source of this belief in equality – indeed, of the necessity of equality – is, in part, philosophical, deriving from the Revolution of Reason, but it has important sociological roots as well, intimately connected with modern society. Mobility, the minute and complex division of labour in society, and the separation of 'work' from 'life' are some of the factors which appear to make it very difficult for people to internalise visions of themselves which imply fixed class or caste differences. As Ernest Gellner has pointed out, 'You cannot be a serf from 10 a.m. to 5 p.m.'[4] The result is a kind of negative value: the demand that citizens be 'like' one another.

The earliest manifestation of the demand for 'likeness' was the demand for equality under the law. To be treated in the same manner before the law was a way of making men more similar. But its sociological thickness is scarcely exhausted by legal equality. Rather, its sociological roots appear to demand a highly visible form of likeness, the empirical and phenomenological facts of likeness. People must actually *be* like one another and *feel* like one another to fully satisfy the modern demand for equality. They must share the same idiom, have similar aspirations and value similar things.

The demand for social 'likeness' manifests itself in contemporary economic demands. The current pressure for decreasing economic differentials, for redistribution of the national product and the heat with which these goals are pursued make little sense unless they are conceived as a barely disguised way of talking about inequality. The issue of 'justice', so often raised in the debate on the New International Economic Order, is not justice in the sense of giving each man his due. Rather, justice has been redefined as 'equal shares' of some mythical international product.

The second, and some would argue, more important manifestation of the demand for likeness is the demand for cultural uniformity. To be truly equal it would appear that people within the same society must share the same culture, speak the same language, in manners and morals as well as in dialect, and value roughly the same things. They must all be able to discourse on roughly equal ground. Otherwise they will not have equal access to society's benefits. In particular, people must share the same culture with their rulers or those in authoritative positions. Hence, modern nationalism and its important part in the contemporary idiom.

The appeal to the Nation is, in function, the contemporary equivalent to the eighteenth-century appeal to the Common Good. It is an appeal to special groups in society to give up privileges for the good of the whole just as it signals a government's intention to serve the whole society, not just particular groups within it.

But the appeal to the Nation goes further than the appeal to the Common Good since, unlike the idea of Common Good, the idea of a Nation is tied up with the idea of a (single) culture, and statesmen can use the appeal to a cultural ideal to impose a commonality of language, dress and habits, to punish deviants, and to give to people of diverse ethnic origins a single cultural standard to which they should conform. Unlike the appeal to the Common Good, nationalism can be used to create among a diversity of people a common culture. Behind it is the demand which modern or modernising societies seem to experience for single-culture societies of shared idiom.

Not all states may appear to be overly concerned with equality, but where they are not, they are generally concerned with the needs of a 'nation' and from one point of view these are not very different concerns. Rather, they are differentially appropriate to societies at different stages of economic and social development. Equality tends to be used in developed societies as an appeal against gross inequalities of class; nationalism tends to be evoked in underdeveloped societies where there are deep differences between ethnic or regional or religious groupings.

Nationalism is not the only leveller in contemporary societies. Socialism performs the same function and in a structurally similar way. Like nationalism, it provides an ideal people – the proletariat; it provides a common language which they can all speak – the language of Marxism-Leninism; it also provides a social programme to weld the 'whole' people together. So, too, may religions serve nationalist functions, particularly when the religion is tied up with a national language and contains a populist element.

But all contemporary nationalisms tend to be similar in one respect; they tend to be tied to secular, technological aims. We might call them 'secular' nationalisms. Their aims are avowedly transitional. They aim to achieve a certain necessary transformation of society which will allow at least the appearance of wider access to its fruits.

The demand for the economic and social manifestations of likeness produces considerable social tension in today's world. In developed societies it must coexist with complex divisions of labour, in underdeveloped societies with their functional realities of caste and tribe. It may even revivify declining tribal awareness, arcane group loyalties and sub-state nationalisms where groups feel disadvantaged. In modern cultures, where erosion has gone quite far, it may lead to the adoption of gratuitous identity-seeking on the part of individuals who feel excluded by the dominant attitudes. It imposes on governments the need for continuous monitoring. But the cure for all this tension is almost invariably seen in carrying the equalisation process still further rather than in reversing it.

If equality and nation-building are the prevalent aims of contemporary societies, the chief means for their achievement in the current idiom is modernisation. Modernisation is a strategy for social change designed to create the ideal society. It outlines a complex programme of interrelated parts, the chief elements of which are industrialisation, bureaucratisation, universal education and secularisation. Each of these is thought necessary to produce some social prerequisite for equality. Together they are intended to create the freedom of physical, spiritual and social movement which appears to be encompassed by our modern notions of what is required for one person to be the equal of another.

We should be wary of treating modernisation as an 'objective' process or as an historical event. The history it purports to describe is highly mythical, while its effects are often unintended and unpredictable. In reality, some societies might seal themselves off from the intrusions of modernity while others can and do adapt old institutions and social forms to personalised forms of partial modernisation and are not 'modernised' at all. Rather than as an objective, historical process, modernisation ought more properly to be understood as an ideal of the good and a goal that is being sought for the benefits it might bring. It ought to be understood, as well, in its intimate relationship to the creation of single-culture societies; in the modern idiom, the two are functionally linked; the one is deemed necessary to create the other.

Modernisation, its progress and requirements, is generally measured by economic criteria. There are other referents which might be used. Mobility, intellectual flexibility and willingness to experiment are all equally signs of being modern. But since these capabilities are seen to be dependent on creating certain minimal economic conditions in society, the present tendency is to subsume them under accounts of GNP and rates of growth. The consequence of this tendency is to turn the economy into the regulator of modernisation and to give to competent economic management a very high value.

But economic growth is a mere tool, not an end in itself, so that, while it is important, its status also allows for the frequent sacrifice of rational economic planning to the needs of social cohesion.

This triad, briefly sketched, of equality, nationalism and modernisation appears to comprise most of the contemporary idiom of legitimacy. It is a remarkably pervasive idiom. It is shared by states at very different levels of development. Few societies appear capable of ignoring this idiom or some of its parts. Even when revolutions are mounted against 'Westernisation', the option to turn back entirely does not seem to be really possible. Rather, it would appear that 'tradition' is being used as a disguised form of protest against the inequalities thrown up by modernisation itself. The Islamic revival in Iran is probably at least as much this form of protest as a real return to the past.

Such mixtures of old and new may inspire confusion in the participants no less than in analysts. Ladies put on veils to attend university; gentlemen pray five times a day while calculating the multiplier effects of some industrial project; social scientists try to calculate the input which ought to be assigned to the Jihad in a rational calculus of the possibilities of future war. The continuation of the old within the framework of the new ought, however, to be treated with caution. Not that the ancient laws of the Jihad are irrelevant – they might indeed emerge as regulators of social behaviour in the old-becoming-new societies. But when they do, it will be in transfigured forms: as direction-givers to mass armies led by technologically sophisticated officers in pursuit of distinctly modern ends.

IDEOLOGY, THE STATE AND MODERN DIPLOMACY

The characteristic state-form produced by this ideology is the centralised, highly bureaucratic state responsible for the performance of an immense variety of tasks, the most important of which are the achievement of social cohesion and economic management. Bureaucracy existed before the development of nineteenth-century social theory but that theory justified its expansion and made possible its characteristic twentieth-century form and its characteristic twentieth-century tasks.

Since the state's tasks are expanded, it is justified in calling upon a larger share of the total resources of society in the carrying out of those tasks. Since it has a larger share of the public resource, it is in a position to mobilise much more power on behalf of its aims. Contrary to successive waves of prediction, the state is not fading away. Rather, it is becoming more extensive and more powerful.

Despite protest and rebellion, it is also becoming more *legitimate*. For what other agency is sufficiently powerful to carry out the tasks implied by modernisation? So long as modernisation is sought after as a positive good, the state machine, as the engine of modernisation, will share in the reflected glow of that positive good.

The difference between the modern state and its predecessors, as is implicitly recognised in the literature on 'transnationalism', is that the modern state does not serve itself. In the present ideology, it serves what appear to be objective, universal goals, and goals that delegitimate a lot of the cultural baggage that the nineteenth-century state relied upon. The modern state cannot rely upon 'Law and Order' or on its constitutional history, at least not entirely, to maintain itself. It is open to continuous judgement by criteria that lie outside the state and can be opposed to it. Hence its apparent weakness, its excessive 'penetrability'. But while particular state machines may fall, they are almost invariably replaced by others which are more pervasive in their duties and, hence, in their rights, and which call upon a steadier and more continuous loyalty from their citizens.

If modernisation depends upon manipulation of the economic machine from within, it correspondingly has justified the state moving to protect the economy from without. The growing force of economic sovereignty, represented by successive draft resolutions at the United Nations, nationalisations of foreign-owned economic plant and claims by states that they are the ultimate arbitrators of the use of natural resources within their boundaries derive from the important role played by the economy in the achievement of social equality and the state's role as monitor of that economy.

Accompanying the drive towards economic sovereignty has been the gradual legalisation of international economic relations, the development of distinctive programmes of economic rights and the tendency towards control of non-state economic actors: foreign individuals as well as multinational companies. In short, the present ideology makes various forms of economic nationalism the norm, and the justifiable norm, so long as the national economy is looked to as the medium by which the transformation of society is to occur.

But it has also justified, indeed created, an imperative for greater economic co-operation among states, and for much the same reason. Since, empirically, the more advanced the state, the more it (except perhaps very large states) will rely on trade and exchange, the more necessary it is seen to be that exchange be stable, and the more states become dependent on the establishment of agreed norms to regulate it. If the state is becoming a business concern, it is also beginning to move within an increasingly complex network of rules as the necessary condition of its own well-being. Hence, the contemporary paradoxical picture of strong states enmeshed in an increasingly tight web of international co-operation. Hence also, that characteristic feature of the modern state system, with us since the onset of industrialisation, the continuing tension between economic nationalism and economic internationalism.

There is much current speculation as to whether protectionism or 'internationalism' will prevail in the future international economy. The point which ought to be made is that they are not real alternatives in the way they appeared to be during the interwar period. Both protectionism and internationalism belong to the same world, each being thrown up in response to some small movement in the modernisation process, in response to one or another of its different requirements. For the present at least, *neither* can sweep the board.

The present common understandings have left a very distinct mark on notions of intervention. On the one hand, the idea of a social transition aimed at bringing a people to genuine political citizenship, awareness and freedom makes interference in that process appear a criminal act, among the worst of all international 'crimes'. Moreover, the expansion of the state's tasks has been accompanied by a widening of the notion of intervention; today, mere influence may be termed intervention.[5] On the other hand, it has also ambiguously justified intervention in those cases where intervention is seen to be aiding a movement whose declared aims are to bring a nation into being. The result of these developments has been to deprive the principle of non-intervention of any legal precision and to make it a highly political and contentious question.

On the institution of war, the effect of modern notions of legitimacy and current social demands have been most dramatic: war has virtually disappeared as an acceptable diplomatic strategy. The justifiable use of war by the state in behest of *state* ends seems to have died with the First World War. It has been replaced by 'police actions', 'interventions', 'collective punishments', 'deterrence'.[6] Force matters, of course, and power differentials have been structured into the state system and institutionalised in a manner unique in its history. But the use of force in the pure form of war appears very difficult without a collectivist intention.

Aside from clear cases where self-defence unambiguously requires pre-emptive attack, the only fully justified initiation of hostilities today is 'people's war', what Michael Walzer has called 'the levée en mass authorised from below'.[7] Moreover, it is a people's war inspired by a particular end. 'War has outlived all its justifications but that of liberty', wrote Hannah Arendt.[8] In other words, only wars of national liberation seem to be just wars.

The increasing legitimation of revolutionary wars can only derive from the view of man and society held in popular legitimacy. For, in the prevailing view, man only becomes man within the context of a certain kind of society. The revolution is an explicit transformational device which brings society from one condition into another. Wars fought in its name and seeming to promise such a transformation cannot be disqualified as viable political movements.

The effect of present common understandings on the institutions of modern diplomacy has been correspondingly profound. Economic diplomacy is one effect of states turned over to economic goals. Another is the extraordinary institutional diffusion of modern diplomacy and the concomitant downgrading of foreign offices. If the entire economic machine is involved in continuous interaction with other economic machines, then the limitation of diplomacy to foreign offices will naturally appear a hindrance to the rational conduct of foreign relations. Yet another is the ease with which new international regimes are established. Indeed, a whole body of 'regime' literature has emerged which views the concept of the 'regime', akin to the notion of contract, as the most viable way of approaching the contemporary state system.[9] But perhaps its most remarkable effect has been the creation, on the one hand, of a heavily *democratic*, indeed parliamentary, framework for present international proceedings and, on the other, somewhat paradoxically, the establishment of special great power responsibilities within that overall framework.

Parliamentary diplomacy is the application of the principle of one-man-one-vote, the first principle of legal equality, to the society of states. The movement to delineate a superordinate position for the great powers within the state system follows the fortunes of the institution of war. It would appear that the more unfeasible war became, in its social as well as material effects, the more power was brought under legal regulation to be exercised through legal channels. But the giving of authority to the great powers is not just a consequence of material destruction, although that is crucial to it. It is also a fact about general social understandings. For what distinguishes the modern age from the Ancien Régime is that society is believed to be going somewhere, and societies which are going somewhere require manipulable structures within which they can move. This creates at once a certain value in maintaining somewhere in the system what some modern political scientists would call a 'leadership function'.

THE STRUCTURES OF GREAT POWER RELATIONS

The formal leadership function of the great powers was established by Chapters VI, VII, VIII and XII of the United Nations Charter which empowered a Security Council to identify threats to the peace and to take action designed to contain those threats. It was enshrined *de facto* in the system of blocs. In the Security Council, the great powers were intended to reflect on the requirements of peace and to hand down their consensus on those requirements to the world at large. Their failure to achieve such a consensus led them into the process of bloc-building. The Security Council remains the arena where they express their agreements vis-à-vis the world at large. The bloc system has become the arena in which they quarrel, moderate their relations with one another and set the terms of their collaboration or lack thereof. The system of blocs displays the Security Council in its dissident aspect.

Of the two, it is the dissidence among the great powers which has most set the tone and shape of the contemporary state system. Indeed, they have tended to use their Security Council status to register and legitimise agreements between the blocs which require more general international action for their implementation, such as the non-proliferation treaty, or their minimal agreements on the Middle East; and 'threats to the peace' are often precisely those threats that disturb the delicate business of managing the blocs.

This intimate connection between the Security Council and the bloc system has tended to elevate agreements reached across the blocs into superordinate agreements for the system at large, as if the Security Council had spoken. In fact, it has not. Such understandings as 'overkill' or the numbers of civilian dead tolerable or the targetting of missiles, which may be vital to deterrence and which are occasionally treated as if they have a quasi-regulatory force for the system as a whole, have no general legal status whatsoever.

At the base of the quarrel between the great powers lies the question of the proper relation between state and society. It is a question which might have been buried or postponed or for which they might have found a compromise had it not been for the necessity of a decision over the reconstruction of Germany. It was the quarrels of the great powers over the future of their wartime enemy which led them to initiate the process of bloc-building; it was the failure to achieve a satisfactory form for that state which led them to complete it. The blocs were to serve as a surrogate and interim framework for a German settlement until a more satisfactory one might be achieved. None ever was; and the system of blocs has itself come to serve as a sort of permanent stand-off.

The limits of movement, between and within the blocs, are measured against the political and military requirements of deterrence. The outlawing of war has scarcely been diminished by the development of nuclear weapons. Rather, nuclear deterrence theory is a body of theory on how to apply nuclear power to war avoidance. Bernard Brodie has called it *utility in non-use*. A feasible deterrent is one which deters, without risk of adventurism, without invitation to surprise attack and without raising political hostility to such a level that confrontation may be provoked. In deterrence theory, weapons are, or ought to be, developed in order to ensure that they will not be used. This would appear to be the only justification for their deployment which is possible.

Occasionally the United States is swept by pressures for more active deterrent postures, involving the enunciation of war-fighting doctrines and theories of nuclear use which picture 'acceptable' nuclear wars. But such pressures and doctrines always inspire protests, anti-nuclear movements and alliance disaffection at levels which have been sufficient to assure, so far at least, the impossibility of their adoption.

The demands of deterrence have led to the establishment of

permanent institutions within each bloc and a permanently institutionalised dialogue between the blocs. Within each bloc's institutional framework, it has required permanent preparedness, close co-ordination on the ends as well as the means of policy and virtually permanent diplomacy. Between them, the function of dialogue is not only to resolve disputes but simply to inform on military developments, strategic thinking and political interests.

Such continuous co-ordination imposes considerable strain on alliance members but dissidence has not yet been carried to the point of alliance disruption. Instead, freedom of manoeuvre against the demands of centralised decision-making has been sought through the elaboration of yet more institutions, such as the European Community, through which is created legal space for greater freedom of action on the part of alliance members.

Apart from their leadership function, in their class as 'ordinary' states, these powers share distinctive economic forms. They are industrialised, democratic and highly bureaucratised, with complex divisions of labour. In other words, they share those characteristics most closely associated with 'modernity'. Modernisation consists for them in *anticipating* the technological and societal forms required to remain modern.

The economic plant of these societies, its viability, requires stable exchange rates, steady access to raw materials, large markets and a mobile labour force. The scale of enterprises mean that these demands must be met in as predictable a form as possible. 'Interdependence' in the current idiom is deemed to be a condition shared more or less equally by all in the modern world; in fact, the most highly industrialised are much more interdependent than the less developed. Moreover, they are interdependent in a particular way. Their need is for the utmost regularity in exchange.

This need can only be met by steady monitoring, by continuous diplomacy and by a high degree of international regulation. Hence, the development of increasingly elaborate international institutions and treaty frameworks for the regulation of trade and money. The European Community, the Groups of Ten and Twenty, the growing practice of economic summits, these are only some of the mechanisms of economic monitoring and economic control. They are flanked by a myriad of others, less public, which touch every aspect of national life in a more or less determinate fashion. Together they link the highly industrialised into a dense framework of economic and functional organisations as exclusive in effect as their political responsibilities and their mutual antagonisms make them by intent.

Despite, and indeed partly because of, this dense network, the highly industrialised are vulnerable to bouts of economic nationalism. As they show the more extreme forms of modernisation, they also display its more extreme political tendencies. Since they are also highly interdependent, these displays are very disturbing making economic nationalism increasingly the concern of all and leading to increasing internationalisation of national concerns and national politics.

The relationship between the structures of political monitoring and those of economic well-being is one of formal separation, but it is unavoidable that they intrude upon one another. If the NATO requires a 3 per cent real growth in defence allocations, the economic performance of its members becomes a vital defence concern.

That they are seen to be related is demonstrated by the establishment of a NATO Committee on the Challenges of Modern Society and by occasional United States efforts to relate them in principle. In 1973 the United States administration, which had been arguing for several years that its heavy world political responsibilities made it eligible for favourable treatment in economic negotiations, proposed to the Europeans that a quasi-formal link between the two be established. But while the claim was acted upon informally, it was strenuously denied in principle; and the formal and legal separation of world political responsibilities and intra-industrial economic relations has been maintained.

THE STRUCTURES OF THIRD WORLD DIPLOMACY

Contemporary social thought has given the Third World less a stable structure of international relations than a structure of fragile states and rhetorical devices. Had they entered upon statehood armed with the theory of the Divine Right of Kings, with its minimal demands on loyalty, their practical tasks might have been easier. But the commitment to development, modernisation and nation-building, with its justification for elaborate state machines distributing extensive funds in the midst of societies where tribe, clan and caste retain important residual functions, has turned the state into a corruption-breeder and a field for contention surpassing even the seventeenth-century European state in instability. Of the 130 wars fought since 1945, 125 have been in the Third World and more than 100 have been anti-regime, tribal, religious, or separatist wars.[10] Third World politics has been aptly characterised as the 'frenzy within the state'.

Their low levels of development and often unstable political orders make them resemble seventeenth-century states in one respect, however. It is the state itself which is the chief obsession of Third World statesmen and the state itself which is their chief framework. Indeed, if the new states were to exist on their own, their institutional environment would probably, in fact, resemble the early modern international system with its egotistical actors, its frequent civil wars, its rapidly shifting alliances and its amorphous but developing system of international law.

Particular states or groups of states still bear the marks of an imperial past and behind their atomised presence in the system lie the residues of diverse imperial relationships, often barely concealed. In the case of Latin America, the combination of introversion and subordination virtually excludes it from participation in the system at large.

The ideology of national development has not served entirely to weaken these links, although it has changed their form. Indeed, it may have strengthened them. Development is the *sine qua non* of political legitimacy to these states. A relationship entitling the underdeveloped to special consideration such as a post-imperial relationship may be one worth fostering. Also, the encouragement of development in a society where the minimal economic activity that exists is tied into the economic structure of the ex-colonial power may lead to a widening of traditional economic ties, despite the desire of most Third World states to demonstrate their independence by diversifying their economic relations. Hence, their continued preoccupation with the dangers of neo-colonialism and the fact that regardless of their diversity former colonies are linked together by a common rhetoric.

But the concern with colonialism does not arise solely from the existence of residual economic links. The combination of internal instability and imperial residue led for some twenty years after the Second World War to an interventionist frenzy as each imperial power tried to protect its global mobility and economic plant through the period of decolonisation.

To weak, self-regarding states, fearful of intervention, whose governments are continually attempting to legitimise their expanded prerogatives, all the traditional instruments of external legitimacy have proved extremely useful. Recognition, non-intereference and rhetorical appeals in respect of all the classic canons of international law are part of the baggage of any new diplomat. But if new states have been unexpectedly conservative with regard to international law, they have also given the classic canons a distinctly modern and, to developed states, an extremist interpretation.[11]

The regional body has proved another and very effective device for Third World statesmen. Regional bodies have been used to preserve unstable regional *status quos*, fend off the dangers of intervention and create the appearance of a seeming independence.

If law and the regional body are the most important instruments in the diplomacy of new states, rhetoric follows a close third. The notion of a transition which is externally evaluated and upon which legitimacy depends makes regular public accountings and public demonstrations of right attitude part of the normal process of gaining and holding political power. The ritual of General Assembly speeches is the contemporary parallel of eighteenth-century protocol rituals.

The stage upon which the rhetoric is employed and the laws are adopted is the UN General Assembly. It is entirely appropriate that contemporary notions of legitimacy should have set about these new creations a structure so adapted to their needs. The institutions of parliamentary diplomacy – of one state, one voice, majority rule, the quasi-legal status of General Assembly resolutions – these form the single most important mode of changing and informing the legal and customary practices of the system at large.

For the Third World the Special Committee on Decolonisation, the UNCTAD and the Special Sessions of the General Assembly have proved particularly useful. Since, as UN bodies, they are formally politically neutral, their reports and resolutions have an important norm-setting function. They are also, by the rules of parliamentary diplomacy, relatively easy of access to Third World states. Both qualities make them important institutions for the realisation of their economic and anti-colonial aims.

These devices have not served to insulate new states entirely from great power attentions. Developing countries are too dependent on funds for development, too politically and militarily weak and too enmeshed in the global interests of the great powers to achieve an often desired insularity. The great powers for their part, if they have particular interests in particular Third World countries, tend to set their requirements of Third World states by the terms of their mutual antagonisms and the needs of bloc politics. It is the terms of their relations with one another which tend to establish the framework of their relations with the Third World, not Third World needs or special relationships.

In the immediate postwar period, John Foster Dulles involved the great powers in a series of overlapping treaty arrangements with key Third World states to prevent Soviet penetration into the Third World. These alliances were conceived by their architect and portrayed as a series of extensions of the NATO alliance; the total structure was referred to as the 'Free World Alliance'; and threat to any of its parts was considered a 'threat across the whole front'. The respective military balance between East and West made it appear not unwise to turn nuclear deterrence into a quasi-universal institution as well, embracing that 'free world'.

The United States and its allies treated the UN during the 1950s in the same light, as a 'free world' institution which existed to protect states against certain unnamed but generally understood threats. The fact that crucial parts of the world were already linked with the great powers in a wide series of bilateral treaty arrangements clearly affected the way they behaved within the UN, with the consequence that it became virtually an extension of the Western Alliance, another of its institutions.

Economic relations were organised in terms of a similar 'one-worldness'. The new economic institutions set up after the war made little special provision for non-industrial countries of the world as a particular class. It was believed, in the idiom of the day, that development was a semi-automatic process which could be accommodated within the IMF–GATT regulations, after a short transitional period. Moreover, the requirements for the 'transition' tended to be defined by cold war criteria and aid allocated accordingly. Thus, the UN, the 'free world' and the postwar economic institutions appeared to be of a piece, each an attribute of the other.

It was in reaction to this highly structured and restrictive framework that the rhetoric of non-alignment was developed. If definitions of non-alignment were always rather empty of positive content, this is not surprising. It was an attempt, relatively successful, to create little more than room for manoeuvre for self-regarding states in a situation of political confinement.

The brinkmanship of the superpowers during the late 1950s and the early 1960s changed that framework in certain quite crucial respects. One of the lessons of brinkmanship, realised after the Cuban crisis, was that the nuclear balance was much too delicate to allow of disturbances or competition in peripheral areas. This understanding led the great powers gradually to differentiate what lay at the centre, geographically and ideologically, of their dispute (it was this understanding which led finally to an interim settlement of the German question), and what could be regarded as peripheral to it. This did not imply an agreement to allow competition in the peripheries. Quite the contrary; it involved a tacit agreement to refrain from involvement, for fear of disturbing the over-strained centre.

In practice, this tacit agreement led to a period of great power aloofness in the Third World, to their moving to seal off disputes, and to individual and not collective initiatives. Interventions dropped off after 1965 and the Europeans consistently refused to accept US involvement in Vietnam as an aspect of the defence of the 'free world', while the Nigerian civil war in 1967, unlike that in the Congo in 1960, was not made the occasion of a political crusade.

The differentiation between centre and peripheries was paralleled, not coincidentally, by the theoretical development in International Relations literature of the concept of the 'subsystem', the semi-autonomous region of the international system with its own concerns and its own political modes of grappling with 'regional' disputes.

These developments shattered the ideological mould of a single world patterned on the alliances and tended to push the alliances back to their European centre. By extension, they freed Third World states from the threat of being cast into the ideological cold. As a consequence, Third World statesmen gained greater freedom of manoeuvre and could carry on normal political intercourse with whomsoever they wished. In these circumstances the functions of the non-aligned movement changed: it became less an instrument for achieving freedom from cold war ideological commitment than yet another instrument through which a whole variety of revisionist claims could be pressed.

The process of political differentiation did not itself produce new thinking about economic development; rather it allowed doubts to come to the fore. For, once the alliances receded, economic development in the Third World was not immediately seen as having necessarily to follow one course or another. A truer separation of political alignments and economic experimentation could be allowed. This meant that Third World development could be considered in its own terms. The result was the crystallisation of particular claims on the part of the developing countries against the existing international economic structures, culminating in the demand for a New International Economic Order.

The effect on the United Nations of this shift has been considerable. It has lead to the virtual take-over of the UN by the Third World and its transformation into *the* agency, if not of development, then certainly of economic dissidence.

In political terms, these changes neutralised the UN to the occasional discomfiture of the United States. Regional and ideological concerns have obtruded to cut across 'free world' concerns and the great powers have found themselves required to jostle for position and influence, to head off unpalatable resolutions from much weaker positions and to accept increasingly the dynamic of sheer numbers.

But if Third World statesmen have discovered greater freedom of manoeuvre within a more flexible international system, if they have available a greater range of political action and more freedom to experiment economically, this is due ultimately to the fact that the great powers found the extension of cold war structures into the Third World a dangerous complication in the management of relations among themselves. Once again, it was the needs of the bloc system which established the range of freedoms available to the Third World.

Looked at as a whole, the present international order establishes the great powers as a special class, economically as well as politically, living in a special world of their own. But it also gives the terms of their relationship a determinate influence over the system as a whole. On the other hand, the strains imposed by modernisation and the achievement of co-culturality, if they are felt differentially by different classes of states, are suffered by them all. Equally, the ideal models of modernisation are not those necessarily displayed by the traditional great powers. Brazil, or Sweden, or Singapore might offer more valid methods of social and economic management. The great powers are more clearly set apart from, and the terms of their relationship have a more determinate influence over, the other members of international society than at any time in the past, but the aims they serve are no longer culturally specific to them. This makes the world look like a global village while, in fact, being a very complex conurbation with its centre and its peripheries in which conceptually similar 'citizens' cohabit in highly differentiated circumstances.

NOTES: CHAPTER I

1   Andrew Orridge has provided a nice account of the spread of the idea of nationalism in 'Varieties of nationalism', in Leonard Tivey (ed.), *The Nation-State* (London: Martin Robertson, 1981). I am indebted to him for reference to a similar account of the spread of the process of modernisation by Reinhardt Bendix: 'Tradition and modernity reconsidered', *Comparative Studies in Society and History*, vol. 9 (1966–7).

2   Less apocryphal is the assessment of Baron von Gneisenau in the aftermath of Jena. 'The Revolution has set the whole strength of a nation in motion, and by the equalisation of the different classes and the equal taxation of property converted the living strength in man, and the dead strength in resources, into a productive capital, and thereby upset the old relations of States. If other States desire to restore this equilibrium, they must appropriate the results of the Revolution.' Quoted by G. P. Gooch, *Germany and the French Revolution* (London: Longman, 1927), p. 533.

3   It has been republished in Martin Wight, *Systems of States*, ed. Hedley Bull (Leicester: Leicester University Press, 1977), pp. 153–73.

4   'Nationalism or the new confessions of a justified Edinburgh sinner', *The Political Quarterly*, vol. 49, no. 1 (January–March 1978), p. 107.

5   See United Nations General Assembly Resolution 2131 (XX) of 21 December 1965 for the most recent, and very wide, definition of intervention.

6   With consequent difficulties for the applicability of laws of war; see J. G. Starke, *An Introduction to International Law* (London: Butterworth, 1977), pp. 554–62, who notes the growth of a special international law governing 'non-war' hostilities.

7   *Just and Unjust Wars* (London: Allen Lane, 1978), p. 180.

8   *On Revolution* (London: Faber, 1963), p. 1.

9   See Robert Keohane and Joseph Nye, *Power and Interdependence: World Politics in Transition* (Boston, Mass.: Little, Brown, 1977) and Oran Young, *Compliance and Public Authority* (Baltimore, Md: Johns Hopkins University Press, 1979).

10 The figures are adapted from Istevan Kende's 'Local wars 1945–76'; in A. Eide and M. Thee (eds), *Problems of Contemporary Militarism* (London: Croom Helm, 1980), pp. 261–85, an updated version of his classic piece, 'Twenty-five years of local wars', *Journal of Peace Research*, vol. VIII, no. 1 (1971).

11 See, especially, the continuous efforts to establish economic sovereignty as a principle in international law, culminating in UN General Assembly Resolution 3281 (XXIX) of 12 December 1974 containing the Charter of Economic Rights and Duties of States.

2
Sovereignty

CHRISTOPHER BREWIN

State sovereignty may be regarded as the counterpart in doctrine to the modern territorial division of the world into legally separate jurisdictions. Its universal reception has greatly simplified international political theory. The origins and rise of state sovereignty have been correlated with an even more remarkable acceptance all over the world of a doctrine of individual sovereignty: while traditional human identifications with tribe or family or religion continue to exist, men and women are almost everywhere formally regarded as equal citizens. From the point of view of the community of states, the doctrines are closely linked in that all states make the historically unusual claim that their legitimacy derives from the 'real' wills of their citizenry. Collectively, states have acknowledged this novel principle of self-determination in instruments such as Article 1 of the United Nations Charter and the General Assembly Resolution 1514 (XV) on decolonisation of 14 December 1960.

The importance of sovereignty to the community of states can be gauged from the fact that it has spread in less than 300 years from its first recognisably modern formulation in England and France to acceptance throughout Europe and now throughout the world. Its continued efficacy is illustrated by the establishing of jurisdiction over the exploitation of air, sea and ocean floor through the extension of the scope of territorial state sovereignty upwards and outwards. The concept remains fundamental to an understanding of international law, international trade, international organisation and diplomacy.

An adequate account even of the contemporary influence of sovereignty on state practice is beyond the scope of this chapter.[1] Instead I want to suggest briefly some ways in which historical understanding can account not only for the sudden reception of the concept but also for the widespread bemusement and hostility which presently accompanies that reception. The near-universality of doubts on the subject of sovereignty has to be expressed and explained. Thus the theorists of the major blocs – Russian Marxists, American pluralists and Third World structuralists – seem united in regarding sovereignty as at best a temporary expedient and at worst a mystification. The idea that the sovereign individual and the sovereign state are the basic units of political theory seems largely confined to Kantians, Gaullists and the English school of international relations. Equally significant is the indifference of many contemporary lawyers to what a long tradition exemplified by Sir Ernest Barker insisted was properly a legal doctrine. For example, the recent work of James Crawford gives scant treatment to sovereignty as 'an incident or consequence of statehood',[2] a matter of rights and duties. Also in both legal and political discourse there is unresolved confusion in Europe, the cradle of the doctrine, where limitations of sovereignty are explicitly envisaged in the postwar constitutions of France and Italy, in the Basic Law of the Federal Republic of Germany, in the judgments of the Court of Justice of the European Community[3] and in the Brezhnev doctrine.

In attempting to resolve this apparent paradox, namely, the near-universal denial of the fundamental importance of sovereignty at the moment of its universal triumph, I shall argue that the same factors can account at once for the reception of sovereignty and for the fragility of that reception, from both a domestic and an international perspective. I shall proceed first by differentiating modern versions of the doctrine from writings on authority in other civilisations before turning more specifically to the domestic origins of the modern theory and its international implications. Finally, and somewhat tentatively, I shall suggest that an additional explanation of the paradox lies in the present state of transition from an international community of states sharing the world to an international society of states characterised by shared rule in certain respects over the world or regions of it.

I

The originality of the modern doctrine of sovereignty is often obscured by attempts to compare it with analogous but fundamentally different conceptions in the city-states of Greece, the Warring States period in China, Roman law or the later Middle Ages. Modern theories of sovereignty, however, are distinctly unlike these earlier understandings of the nature of authority in two ways. The first is in the link between individual and state sovereignty in modern theory; the second lies in the claim by modern states to be the sole arbiter of law within their territories.

Aristotle began with the economic unit of the household and Confucius with the hierarchical duties of family members. It is a peculiarity of the Western concept of state sovereignty that it is closely tied to a notion of individual sovereignty or citizenship. This reflects the practice of modern states and modern employers in taxing, conscripting and employing individuals rather than villages or family units.

With hindsight it is clear that this correlation of state with individual sovereignty has been present since the writings of Bodin and Hobbes. But the novelty of the doctrine may be underlined by consideration of the medieval trappings of their arguments. Thus Bodin's justification of untrammelled royal power is based on an analogy with a master's rightful power over his household. The few 'masterless men' of sixteenth-century England and France were regarded as a social problem and not as the obvious units of political theory: Bodin's contemporary Marlowe was making a scandalous break with medieval drama when he wrote a play about an individual peasant called Tamburlaine who made himself into an emperor. Hobbes's initial chapters, 'Of Man', are more accessible to us precisely because of their Cartesian individualism and the Protestant possibility of an unmediated relationship with God. What we sometimes fail to notice is that Hobbes's sovereign individuals were heads of households. Hobbes excluded servants from contractual status so naturally that he did not have to argue the point.

Interesting as the correlation of individual citizenship with individual state sovereignty is in itself, it is more significant that it is seldom noted. Like the dog which did not bark in Sherlock Holmes's story, this has to be explained. Hobbes's writings themselves provide two clues.

The new kind of unlimited rule he sought to establish was limited in territorial extent so naturally that he rarely mentioned the words England, Holland, or France. To paraphrase C. B. Macpherson, Hobbes assumed an existing community of Englishmen who shared the tradition, the land, the interests already celebrated in Shakespeare's more patriotic plays. It follows that there can be a relationship between the autonomy of individuals and the autonomy of states precisely because theorists assume an existing community. These communities may be formed over time by a blood relationship, or by being ruled by the same kingdom or empire, or by all the other causes of those nationalisms which have bound together in new forms the individuals atomised by the breakdown of pre-modern communities. Such communities may be divided by classes or factions or interests but as units they are sufficiently united to be capable of being ruled or of ruling themselves. Until very recently there was no similar community of states uniting the whole world. Hence one will not find either in Hobbes or in subsequent writings much attention to the formula: as the individual is to the state, so the state is to the world. The 'security' logic in *Leviathan* specifically did not require a compact among sovereigns for Hobbes argued that states unlike individuals were not subject to sudden and complete destruction.

In addition to the assumption of community Hobbes provides a second clue to the problem of the relation between sovereign individual and sovereign state. Hobbes's citizen shared a community but did not share rule, except for the anachronistic medieval relic that the sovereign king or republican assembly should pay heed to counsel. The citizen is almost forgotten once it has been demonstrated that he had better give up his right to all things to a sovereign politician who will rule on what the law is and what God says. The only residue of the individual's autonomy was the right to resist when personally attacked by sovereign power. In short, Hobbes located sovereignty in a part of the community, the sovereign king or sovereign assembly. The citizens were so far deprived of any say in rule that Hobbes required them to obey any new sovereign who succeeded by war or revolution in replacing the incumbent. He would have approved of the actions of the Polish peasantry in 1789 in being as unconcerned about the Partitions of Poland as were the cattle they tended.

The contrast with the modern world is striking. Today all Poles think of themselves as citizens who ought to have a say in the running of their country, with the consequent problems of refugees and struggles for liberty which aptly illumine the originality of the individual's present identification with the state. Sovereignty since Rousseau has been most often identified with the inalienable right of the whole community to do as it wills. This goes further than Althusius who argued against Bodin that sovereignty should be attributed to the people, a part of the community contrasted with the king. And it goes further than the Grotian compromise that, as sight might be an attribute both of the body and the eye, so sovereignty might be attributed at the same time to the ruler and the people, for in the Grotian theory sovereignty was a form of alienable property. Rousseau's solution of the problem of locating sovereignty between individual and state is as bold as it is difficult to operationalise. French history since the Revolution has been a confusing succession of alterations between 'monarch' and 'assembly' each claiming to mediate the will of the sovereign French people.

This relationship between individual and state sovereignty presupposes the growth among atomised individuals of a sense of a community which is self-consciously trying to rule itself as a political society. It is interesting to note that this understanding of sovereignty was most strongly held in nineteenth-century liberal and nationalist movements. In this century it might be argued there has been a return in Marxist and pluralist thought to attributing rule to a part of the community conceived as more capable of rule than the community as a whole. Thus in Marxist thought it is the bourgeoisie or the dictatorship of the proletariat which is sovereign. And in pluralist thought it is the real decision-makers on any particular issue who matter, and distinctions are made between legal, political and sociological sovereignty.[4]

The second originality of modern doctrine is that the sovereign makes law by his own will. In principle new law may set aside tradition, whether divine law or natural law or human law. Sovereign individuals may make a new contract. Even if, as in the theories of Savigny or Gierke, communities have been formed by organic historical growth, as societies they may decide to depart from their traditions.

There is no parallel to this claim in the Hellenic community of city-states. This is worth stressing as Toynbee and others overlook this point in drawing parallels between modern and earlier sovereign state-systems.[5] It is true that Plato does come very near to the modern view in this passage from *The Republic*:

'it will be necessary that there shall always be present in the city a class possessing that insight into the principles of the constitution in the light of which you, Glaucon, the lawgiver, laid down its laws'.[6]

Nevertheless, it is because Plato's lawgivers are imbued with the rational and eternal principles to which laws ought to conform that they themselves can be set above the laws. Modern sovereigns are not bound by such principles.

The same point can be made with regard to the Roman Empire. The axiom '*Quod principi placuit, legis habet vigorem*' appears to conform with the absolute modern view. Indeed Hobbes's model, King Henry VIII, is said to have established a chair of Civil Law so that this aspect of Roman law could be invoked in asserting royal supremacy over the church. But part of the Roman tradition was the republican insistence that laws of the state in conflict with natural law 'no more deserve to be called laws than the rules a band of robbers might pass in their assembly'.[7] This high view of the superiority of natural law is incompatible with the modern idea of untrammelled legislative authority.

Again, some writers have traced sovereignty back to the medieval period. Martin Wight, for example, quotes Figgis approvingly: 'There was no doubt that the canonists meant by the [Pope's] *plenitudo potestas* everything that the modern means by sovereignty.'[8] While the canonists did come closer to modern ideas than other medieval thinkers the point is that no medieval writer could put the authority to make law beyond the restraints of the laws of God, of the Church, of Nature and of Nations. When Hobbes took each of these traditional restraints on politicians and transformed them into bulwarks of sovereign authority he was being deliberately revolutionary.

The contrast between modern ideas and the practices of traditional societies is well illustrated in the treaties made by colonialists with chiefs who could neither understand nor rightfully will away the sovereignty which was conveniently if temporarily attributed to them.

Lord Lugard's biographer, Margery Perham, asserts his great regard for the principle of sovereignty in examples like this one, at Kishi:

'[Lugard] explained clause by clause, in his conscientious way, what this agreement would mean. Even as he had the standard treaty form translated, Lugard admitted to himself that it was 'pretty stiff'. It asked for the cession of the territory to the Company with full rights of jurisdiction while offering in return a very qualified protection. However the councillors listened eagerly to each word of the treaty – how much of its meaning, even with the explanations, could they understand? – and agreed that it was all good and Lugard went back to his camp at midnight by the light of the moon well pleased with his night's work.'[9]

Such a radically new departure was peculiarly impossible for primitive communities where the emphasis on traditional rights and duties at least balanced the wilfulness of leaders. This is well argued in de Jouvenel's work on sovereignty in which he suggests that authority in primitive communities could be said to be often divided between a leader (Dux) and the embodiment of tradition (Rex).[10]

There is only one exception that I have discovered to this general absence of any doctrine equivalent to the modern originality in stressing the untrammelled nature of sovereign will. Shang Yang (died 338 BC) declared: 'To govern one can follow a different way: as long as it suits the state one need not follow the ancient example.'[11] I do not know enough of the history of the Warring States period to know if in context this is as absolute a rejection of the old ways as its modern Chinese interpreters claim.[12] But it is significant for the argument of the next section that Shang Yang closely resembles modern leaders in his willingness to make wide-ranging and deliberate decisions about basic social, economic and legal arrangements.

II

How and why did this break with the past occur in the West? My working assumption is that doctrines are received and developed because they fit social requirements, whose development is in turn influenced by the doctrine. My thesis is that the doctrinal originality of sovereignty was made possible by the beginning of a long and uneven social process which we label atomisation, and the doctrine became more rigorous in line with a growing need for a legal authority untrammelled in its scope for making rapid and deliberate social changes. Although the theory of 'Leviathan' could be formulated in the seventeenth century it was not accepted as a university textbook until the nineteenth century, when industrialisation required an unprecedented emphasis on authority and coercion as the criteria of law. As the forces of production, the size of markets, the requirements of defence and the management of money have all outgrown the territorial limits of English and French jurisdiction, sovereignty has become less appropriate to domestic conditions and less received as a doctrine for university study.

Thus the formulation of the modern doctrine is correlated with the development of 'territorial market societies' in Western Europe. In the seventeenth century the medieval confusion of jurisdictions and hierarchies was replaced by a single royal jurisdiction. Tolls were abolished. Baronial and urban militias were downgraded. The twin attributes of sovereignty became a monopoly of force and a monopoly of the coinage. 'With the triumph of the kings came the word sovereignty to crystallize what had been achieved.'[13] Externally the claims of papacy and empire were limited by the principle acknowledged at Westphalia of territorial boundaries delimiting religious orthodoxy.

In the eighteenth century the commercialisation of agriculture on the basis of individual tenure was deliberately legitimised in the Enclosure Acts and the edicts of the French Revolution. Blackstone's contemporary theory is correspondingly clear on the importance of a concept of sovereign authority. In every politically organised society, he wrote, there must be present 'a supreme, irresistible, absolute, uncontrolled authority in which the *jura imperii* or rights of sovereignty reside'.[14] But he adds that law was not valid if it transgressed natural and divine law. This continued respect for traditional limitations in the eighteenth century was reinforced by the conservative arguments of Swift and Burke. On this view too, even Rousseau's theory appears in a new light. Concerned with legitimacy, not effectiveness, the sovereign people are untrammelled in what they may decide to do; but, because they all have to be present at the vote, the legislative volume of modern states would be impossible. It is a theory for a territorially small and static society, not for a large and dynamic one.

It is therefore with nineteenth-century industrialisation and twentieth-century revolutions that theorists achieve the greatest rigour in asserting the atomisation of individuals and an untrammelled coercive sovereign authority. 'One man, one vote', Factory Acts and welfare legislation become the order of the day.

Austin in England and Gierke in Germany might be cited as the most influential expounders of a doctrine of sovereignty which legitimised this new scope for self-conscious change. Austin dismisses all 'naturalist' restrictions on coercive authority; and Gierke insists that communities are real collective persons in which the national organic community has 'a sovereign will, absolutely universal, determined only through itself'.[15] In the twentieth century the utility of sovereignty to leaders pushing through revolutionary changes within a given territory in the face of internal resistance and external threat is enough to explain the otherwise anachronistic emphasis on sovereignty in Bolshevik Russia, in Maoist China, in postwar Eastern Europe and in the decolonised states of Asia and Africa. Within countries which have been torn apart by ideological, social and international pressures the sovereign state can of itself provide a focus of unity and decision. In France itself this was part of the appeal of Gaullism, whose unusually successful stress on sovereignty in turn provoked attacks on the doctrine by the General's opponents. And in a world which is radically various in its beliefs, there could not have been the changes in social, economic, military and administrative structures carried out in the last hundred years if there had not been the concept of discrete territorial arenas of sovereign authority.

If this necessarily superficial analysis goes some way in accounting for the importance of sovereignty it also helps to explain current confusion and doubts. For the industrialisation and revolutionary changes which have favoured a rigorous account of sovereignty have themselves extended the arenas appropriate for production, marketing and defence and thereby made existing political arenas less appropriate for decision-making.

These developments have led to a proliferation of functional agencies, regional agencies and 'international' companies and treaties like the Treaty of Rome in which joint rule by states has been in practice required. But there has been no parallel development of the theory of sovereignty which would treat Europe or the world as a political society of states. Instead the reaction has been that typified by Harold Laski, who might be said to represent modern thought in that he was influenced as much by Marxism as by pluralism and was also a consistent advocate of decolonisation. In *The Grammar of Politics* (1925) he wrote that 'it would be of lasting benefit to political science if the concept of sovereignty were abandoned'. More subtly, in his later *Reflections on the Revolution in Our Time* (1943), he accepted the continued domestic importance to existing societies of sovereignty while anticipating its future abrogation as inappropriate to producing either plenty or peace:

'There were thinkers, like Professor Gilbert Murray, who argued that the main need was to abrogate sovereignty; an argument which assumed that the sovereignty of the state is like a tap which can be turned on or off at will, instead of seeing that the sovereignty of the state is an instrument for protecting a given system of productive relations, and that only a revolutionary change in these makes it politically possible to abrogate the sovereignty of the state.' (p. 206)

It is surely significant that, with the exception of nationalism, the ideologies that accompany present large-scale changes – socialism, communism, capitalism, functionalism, structuralism, pluralism and even fascism – are all internationalist in taking what Wallerstein calls the 'world economy' as the unit of explanation.[16]

The increasing importance of international relations to sovereignty might be illustrated by contrasting England and France with Tuvalu, which became in 1978, the latest recruit to the international community. Sovereignty in England and France developed out of internal causes. Even the assertion that the king was emperor in his own dominions with its rejection of papal and imperial claims was a domestic act. But in the case of Tuvalu it might well be asserted that its reception of sovereignty owes more to external than to internal factors. It is to this growth in the importance of international society as a source of the modern reception of the doctrine of sovereignty that I now briefly turn.

III

It was not until the eighteenth century with the beginnings of the problem of 'recognition' beyond Christendom that the international community became directly involved in according rights of sovereignty. 'Sovereignty, in its origin merely the location of supreme power within a particular territorial unit, necessarily came from within and therefore did not require the recognition of other States or princes.'[17] I do not intend here to enter the controversy between the declaratory and constitutive theories of recognition. For both schools in the nineteenth century and in the first part of this century there were no rules determining what were 'states' which could override the discretion of existing states. Crawford quotes Oppenheim's dictum that 'a State is, and becomes an International Person through recognition only and exclusively' even where the criterion for recognition was effective authority. Since sovereignty is a legal status rather than a fact, it follows from the discretionary power of recognition of established states that international law was not formally a complete or coherent system of law. What is interesting is that today lawyers assume that it is a complete system, not only in regard to nationality and the use of force but also at least arguably in respect of rules for establishing statehood. If I have understood this development correctly, lawyers can now equate international society more easily with domestic systems in which the parties are less to be regarded as self-willed Leviathans and more as members of a society akin to citizens within states. The trend to conceiving sovereignty more as a bundle of rights and duties with respect to other similar states is another indication of this change. I suggest but cannot prove that instead of being perceived as a relationship between the state and a particular territory, sovereignty is rather perceived as a social relationship between states where each recognises the rights of others. Similarly, from small beginnings in the nineteenth-century international regulation of waterways, the new regimes in the air, on the ocean floor and with regard to fishing rights might be cited as evidence, although not conclusive evidence, of this development.

International legal thought has also been influenced by political and military developments. Politically the collective influence of the international community on the establishment of new sovereign authorities and the maintenance of the territorial integrity of existing states is itself a novelty. Woodrow Wilson with regard to Eastern Europe and Franklin Roosevelt with regard to European colonies successfully argued that the community of nations should declare active support for self-determination as the proper criterion of the legitimacy of sovereign authority. The increase since 1945 in the number of sovereign states has been associated with even stronger declarations such as the General Assembly Resolution on decolonisation already cited. There was no equivalent community interest in the nineteenth-century comedies enacted in West Africa when rival British and French NCOs planted flags and made treaties in accordance with the ideas of Bodin and Hobbes.

Militarily, the association of increasingly destructive warfare and the sovereign-state system has led to the strongest attacks on the doctrine and arguably a greater collective interest of the community of states in questions of war and peace. This association is deeper than the tautological point that wars are distinguished from other forms of fighting by the characteristic that they are only fought between sovereign units or, in the case of civil war, for the establishment of a different sovereign authority over a unit of unchanged territorial integrity.

Treitschke's robust view of sovereignty provides a good starting-point from which to identify its character:

'Legally it lies in the competence to define the limits of its own authority, and politically in the appeal to arms . . . A defenceless state may still be termed a kingdom for conventional or courtly reasons, but science, whose first duty is accuracy, must boldly declare that in point of fact such a country no longer ranks as a State.'[18]

While many may think that Tuvalu only ranks as a state for courtly reasons, few would be consistent enough to argue that only a state which can defend itself against all comers fulfils the criteria required for sovereign status. The implication would be to restrict the term to the

USA and the USSR and regard their relationship to their 'allies' as one of suzerainty, requiring respect, and possibly tribute of men and money in return for protection. To my knowledge no theorist has maintained the link between sovereignty and Hobbes's image of the fortress-state by taking this radical step.

Instead the development of warfare into world war and the liability of all to involvement in general war has led to a more confused reaction. On the one hand the continued arming of most states may be said to maintain the link between military might, internal and external prestige, and the attribution to sovereign states of a monopoly of the means of violence. On the other hand there has been created a plethora of international organisations. Some aim specifically at the furtherance of peace through joint action or declarations. The European Community, for example, owes its existence to the experience of the world wars. Many publicists have taken the warlike consequences of an ungovernable sovereign-state system as the ground for their attacks on the idea of sovereignty. Toynbee contrasted the wars and susceptibility to barbarian conquest of Sumer and Akkad with 3,000 years of Pharaonic stability in Egypt.[19] And Mitrany's functionalism was also inspired by the desire to reduce the likelihood of war between states who inefficiently concentrated all functions within their separate territorial jurisdictions.[20]

Further evidence of the confused reactions to the scale of modern warfare is provided by reassertions of the previous limitations on sovereignty inherent in natural and divine law which have been most marked on the question of war. The Nuremberg judgement asserts that it is wrong to obey properly constituted sovereign authority when its objective is genocide which goes against natural law and the law of nations. And the twentieth-century permission to conscientious objectors is a development of the Quaker invocation of God's will as a superior limitation on state authority. Inevitably, however, since they are not anchored in any generally held philosophy, such claims remain open to question.

IV

At this stage it may be helpful to summarise the argument. The originality of modern doctrines of the right to rule lies in two aspects – the atomisation of human collectivities into individual units under the rubric of citizenship, and the untramelled authority of political societies within their territories. The importance of this doctrine in its modern form lies in its functional utility to political societies engaged in deliberate and fundamental reform of their social, economic, military and administrative structures. At the same time, the extent of these changes, and in particular the gap that has opened up as a result of them between economic and military, and political structures, has introduced an element of confusion which constantly threatens to undermine the intellectual foundations of the doctrine, although it never quite succeeds in doing so. Meanwhile a parallel and related development has occurred in the international realm: the universal triumph of the modern doctrine of sovereignty has served the cause of the expansion of the community of states, although so dramatic a change in the political landscape has also led to uncertainty and confusion about the consequence of this triumph. The manifestations of this confusion can be found, for example, in the attacks on the doctrine by those who place a high value on distributive justice and see a link between sovereignty and a system of neo-colonial exploitation; or in similar attacks by those who locate the fundamental cause of war in state sovereignty.

Because it is useful, however, the doctrine has survived. Against this background, therefore, we must finally ask what limits can be placed on the sovereign state in a world in which the reception of its central justifying doctrine receives such an ambiguous reception. In this final section I want to suggest that this question can best be answered in terms of R. G. Collingwood's account of the relation between community and society.[21]

According to Collingwood, both the concept of community and the concept of society involve sharing. For a community of states to exist, something must be shared by those states. The international community might be said to share the world. It also shares certain conceptions. For our purposes the present community is unusual in that it shares the whole world among sovereign states whose authority is virtually untrammelled within their specified territorial arena. Moreover there is a shared conception that citizens are the sole source of rights and that communities of citizens are entitled to self-determination if they so will and can realise it. It shares also a weak notion of humanity as requiring states to contribute to the care of refugees, the development of world health schemes for eradicating smallpox, and so forth. In certain parts of the world states form self-conscious communities in that they recognise a common ideology or, as in Europe, share a common cultural heritage, economic and defence interests, and institutions.

Following Collingwood, a society is a community where what is shared is rule. In Cicero's classic definition of a political society it is 'not any collection of human beings brought together in any sort of way but an assemblage of people in large numbers associated in an agreement with respect to justice and a partnership for the common good'.[22]

Communities of citizens become political societies when they succeed in ruling themselves. Successful political societies need as their basis strong community ties in which they share other things beside rule –

land, history, interests, and so on. No society can ever divorce itself from its community basis and every society risks returning to a mere community basis if it ceases to share rule among its members.

From this perspective it is possible to pick up Carr's point that in the twentieth century the problems of change implicit in industrialisation and unemployment, war and revolution, the exploitation of oceans and airspace, go beyond the boundaries of liberal state theory expounded by Bodin, Hobbes and Rousseau.[23] On a worldwide as on a regional basis these problems can only be resolved by joint rule.

This distinction between society and community based on the criterion of the presence or absence of shared rule has, of course, appeal to a writer on sovereignty which is precisely about the right to rule. Beyond this it seems clearer than Tönnies's familiar distinction between shared feelings as the criterion of community and shared contractual links as the criterion of society.[24] For example, is the European Economic Community a community because of shared feelings or more properly a Society of States united by contractual obligations in public international law? Collingwood's distinction is more dialectical. Europe can properly be described as a community of peoples or of states to the extent that peoples or states share traditions, interests, or outlook. At the same time, the European Economic Community members are trying to form a society where rule is joint in certain matters, a society which is constantly threatening to be no more than a mere community.

Collingwood's criterion also throws considerable light on Manning's argument that international society is like a club, formed by resemblance among its members in that each becomes eligible by virtue of its sovereign status.[25] The notion of eligibility is included to account for two facts. On the one hand sovereign states may decide not to participate in international society, as in the examples of Albania and Burma. On the other hand the members may exclude a state from participation, as the United Nations did for a time with Germany, Japan and Communist China by the device of not recognising that the states concerned were sovereign according to the principle of self-determination. Eligibility does get round these difficulties but its awkwardness is unnecessary. For resemblance is decided by an observer while the essence of both community and society is participation, sharing 'x' in the case of community, and sharing rule as well as 'x' in the case of a community which is turning itself into a society. It is a philosophical axiom that resemblance of itself cannot be or involve sharing. It follows that membership in the international community is determined by the sharing of values and interests and membership of international society by sharing rule. When British India or post-Hitlerite Germany or Communist China participated as autonomous states in decisions they became members of international society. This also accounts for the fact that international companies may be subjects of international law and important in the international community without being members of international society, for they do not make law. Collingwood's distinction thus goes deeper in accounting for Manning's description of the distinctive nature of international society. And because it relies less on sociological existentialism with its stress on the wilfulness of member-states it is more possible to conceive of states, like persons, as being essentially members one of another.

When posed directly as a question of rule, the problem confronting states becomes the familiar constitutional problem of reconciling formally equal and historically unequal individuals so that they may act together. It is the problem posed by the social contract tradition. 'The co-existence of wills under some form of order is only possible under a condition of *Recht* – the sum of the conditions under which the will of the individual may be united with the will of all, according to a general law of freedom.'[26]

Of course the answer given by both Kant and Rousseau was that a general law of freedom constitutionally enforceable against states was impossible. The only expedient might be defensive Confederations or Leagues. But since their day the unit of production and defence has outgrown the confines of the historically formed communities of European nationalities. And if the functional argument of this chapter is correct there is ground for the present experiments of attempting joint rule on regional and functional bases.

In conclusion, there is a community of states in that each state has a recognised share of the earth, and the right to make laws within its territory. But as the content of this right is seen to be more formal than real, the stark alternatives are to rely on autarky and renounce involvement with others, or to accept and further the process of turning this community into a real society whose members can jointly make rules, sue and be sued, as the best way of securing the freedom and sovereignty of each.

NOTES: CHAPTER 2

1 This is the subject of a forthcoming book by Professor A. M. James to be published by Faber.
2 J. Crawford, 'The criteria for statehood in international law', in *British Year Book of International Law* (1976–7), p. 139.
3 See for example Cour de Justice des Communautés Européennes, *Recueil, Vol. X*, Costa v. E.N.E.L., affaire 6/64, p. 1159.
4 See J. Dickinson, 'A working theory of sovereignty', *Political Science Quarterly*, vol. XLIII, no. 4; vol. XLIII, no. 1.
5 A. J. Toynbee, *Experiences* (London: Oxford University Press, 1969).
6 Quoted in M. Foster, *Masters of Political Thought*, Vol. 1 (London: Harrap, 1947), p. 64.

7   ibid., p. 183.
8   M. Wright, *Systems of States* (Leicester: Leicester University Press, 1977), p. 131.
9   M. Perham, *Lugard, the Years of Adventure* (London: Collins, 1956), p. 506.
10 B. de Jouvenel, *Sovereignty* (Cambridge: Cambridge University Press, 1957), pp. 98–101, 299–300.
11 Quoted in *Peking Review*, 22 February 1974, p. 6.
12 ibid.
13 J. Dickinson, 'A working theory of Sovereignty', *Political Science Quarterly*, vol. LXII, no. 4, p. 528.
14 G. Jones (ed.), *Selections from Blackstone's Commentaries* (London: Macmillan, 1973), p. 36.
15 Quoted in C. E. Merriam, *History of the Theory of Sovereignty since Rousseau* (New York: Columbia University Press, 1900), p. 117.
16 I. Wallerstein, *The Modern World System* (New York: New York Academic Press, 1974), p. 7.
17 J. Crawford, 'The criteria for statehood in international law', op. cit., p. 96.
18 H. von Treitschke, *Politics*, trans. B. Dugdale and T. de Bille (London: Constable, 1916), Vol. 1, pp. 29–30.
19 A. J. Toynbee, *Mankind and Mother Earth* (New York: Oxford University Press, 1976), p. 55.
20 D. Mitrany, *A Working Peace System* (London: Royal Institute of International Affairs, 1943).
21 R. G. Collingwood, *The New Leviathan* (Oxford: Clarendon Press, 1947), Part II.
22 Cicero, *Republic*, Book I, XXV.
23 E. H. Carr, *Conditions of Peace* (London: Macmillan, 1942), p. 108.
24 F. Tönnies, *Community and Association*, trans. P. Loomis (London: Routledge & Kegan Paul, 1955).
25 C. A. W. Manning, *The Nature of International Society* (London: Macmillan, 1975), pp. 102 ff.
26 I. Kant, *Metaphysical Elements of Justice*, trans. J. Ladd, (New York: Bobbs-Merrill, 1965), p. 34.

3

Nationalism

BRIAN PORTER

I

Nationalism is today the most potent and pervasive of all political doctrines, in process of creating new human groupings, consolidating older ones and having the most profound effects upon the relations and characters of states. In any discussion of the international community, the reality of, or prospects for, such a community, the influence of nationalism cannot be ignored. Does it bring mankind together, and if so, in what sense? Or does it set mankind apart, and again, if it does, in what sense?

These questions are not new. They have been asked since political thinkers first became intellectually aware, in the course of the eighteenth century, of those various developments in social outlook and behaviour to which we conveniently give the name of nationalism. But although the questions have persisted, the answers have varied greatly. Nationalism is not a phenomenon that it is easy to appraise, nor one on which there can be any unanimity of judgement. It has meant different things in different places, at different times and to different people. There are those who have seen it as the great hope of mankind, and there are others for whom it has been a poison in man's collective mind.

Central to any discussion of nationalism is the concept of the nation. This may be said to exist in two senses: as an idea, and as a body of people possessed of that idea. This difference is fundamental. In many new states where a national consciousness has barely arisen, the idea of the nation may be believed in, and acted upon, by a comparatively few people. In such cases it may be many years, perhaps several generations, before the idea of the nation, involving all the values, traditions, assumptions and claims which belonging to that nation entails, becomes the common possession and heritage of the population of the state concerned. When this happens we may say that the nation has an objective reality, that it is a people with a shared view of itself, 'a collective self-image', differentiating it from other peoples.

This national self-consciousness may arise in a variety of ways, but the resultant 'nation' will fall into one of two types: the 'culture nation' derived from an awareness of cultural or linguistic uniqueness; and the 'state nation' derived from a shared historical experience as provided, fostered, and even enforced, by a common government, law and administration, reinforced now and then by the sort of heightened experience that war can give.

States, however, are often the crucibles in which 'culture nations' are formed. The linguistic diversity of medieval England, or of nineteenth-century Italy, gave way to linguistic homogeneity only because of the overwhelming influence that the state, its administration and commerce, have upon language, and, in the latter instance, the process is still far from being complete. Indeed, behind many 'culture nations' which have survived as minorities in larger states is often to be found an historic, former state whose influence has persisted and whose memory is cherished. Such were Hungary and Bohemia in the Austrian Empire, Poland in the Russian, and Scotland in the United Kingdom. In those states which have embraced alien minorities, a new national 'idea' will begin to form, much influenced by the traditions and culture of the majority nation, and will consolidate its hold as the new state undergoes its own historical experiences. Thus the idea of the 'British' nation gradually developed amongst the constituent peoples of the United Kingdom. Common experiences helped them to develop a shared view of themselves, and monuments to Nelson, hero not of an English but of a British victory, were set up in the three capitals.

That Dublin's column to Nelson no longer exists is symbolic of what can happen if the adoption of the new national idea is only partially realised. The older sense of national identity may be sharpened by the threat presented by the new, and the new may be adopted on only one side of a class barrier. Thus an indigenous upper class may become identified with an alien culture, as has to some extent happened in Scotland and Wales, but occurred more particularly in Ireland.

Indeed 'culture nations', which once were vulnerable to the moulding, integrative effects of states, have become markedly resistant to change in an age of nationalism. Nationalism is the philosophy which makes of the nation the fount of values, the focus of loyalty and even, in extreme cases, the object of worship. As an impetus to political action, nationalism will normally lead to national self-determination on the part of the culture nation, and cultural homogeneity on the part of the state nation. Where, therefore, culture nation and state nation do not coincide, they will usually be found in mutual tension.

Where they are not so found, the circumstances of adhering to the multinational or transnational state must be so advantageous, so compelling, that even the desire for national self-determination is put into abeyance – or rather it takes an unexpected turn. With great perceptivity Ortega y Gasset has suggested that nations are less influenced by a remembered past than by an assumed future, and that if a multinational state becomes the vehicle for some great collective enterprise, then the attractiveness of joining in this will outweigh the desire to 'go it alone'. He writes:

'Before all, the State is a plan of action and a programme of collaboration. The men are called upon so that together they may do something. The State is neither consanguinity, nor linguistic unity, nor territorial unity, nor proximity of habitation. It is nothing material, inert, fixed, limited. It is pure dynamism – the will to do something in common – and thanks to this the idea of the State is bounded by no physical limits.'[1]

But from this it follows that if the state holds out no such hopes, if its dynamism has gone, or it appears to belong to some past rather than future order of things, then its constituent peoples will wish to desert it, and will do so unless restrained by force.

This diagnosis would seem to explain much that otherwise appears puzzling. Why did Imperial Germany embark upon a deep water policy when every strategic argument was against it? Why is the Soviet Union now following a remarkably similar course? Could it be that such activities help to bind together unions of rather disparate parts? Indeed, the German navy programme was termed '*Sammlungspolitik*' ('rallying policy'), it being held that whereas the army was predominently 'Junker' and Prussian, the navy could be associated with a broader social class and with the entire German nation. As for the Soviet Union, like the United States, it represents also a great experiment in social organisation, the potentiality of which is still being proved. This alone may be sufficient to counteract the centrifugal forces of national diversity within. Had the Austro-Hungarian Empire embodied some great new enterprise or challenging ideology, there might have been less inducement on the part of its Slavonic provinces to desert a state in which they saw a mighty past but certaintly no future, and desert it despite the advantages that a continued economic union of the Danube basin would undoubtedly give them. Perhaps, too, as one scholar has ingeniously suggested, the building of the pyramids, by far the greatest engineering achievement of antiquity, was not unconnected with forging socially and psychologically the recently obtained political union of Upper and Lower Egypt.[2] If this is a valid insight, we may expect the European Community, if it is to survive, to embark on some course which will inspire enthusiasm on the part of its populations. The 'bandwagon' effect, as well as the 'sinking ship' effect, would certainly seem to be prime influences in the making or breaking of states. And if the state is nationally homogeneous, then the breaking might well take the form of civil war, as the Wars of the Roses followed the failure of England's great enterprise in France.

II

So far we have examined the subtle relationship that one finds between state and nation; how nations fill states, fracture them, form them; how nations are formed by them, and survive despite them. What, we may now ask, are the implications of this relationship for international society as a whole?

This society, now one of states, was originally a society of princes belonging to a common civilisation and emerging from a common universalist feudal order. These princes were not nationalists but dynasts, exploiting nationalism, where it existed, for their own dynastic ends. Their sense of 'class' interest was strong, and it was usual for them to intermarry. To an extent, they shared and cultivated a cosmopolitan culture which marked them off from the peoples whom they ruled.

With the decay of feudalism, dynasticism began to lose its economic basis, and as economic, and eventually political, power passed to new classes of society, so these classes came to adopt nationalism as an ideology which could be employed against the old cosmopolitan dynastic order. Youth, too, and especially youth infused with the ideals of nascent romanticism, took nationalism as its creed, and Rousseau, Herder and Fichte for its prophets.[3] The French Revolution stimulated the process in two ways. It was the aim of the Revolutionary armies to release the nations of Europe from royal and aristocratic bondage, and to establish a 'universal Republic' enshrining and protecting the Rights of Man. And it was the design of Napoleon to create broadly national states to be ruled by his brothers and marshals under the aegis of himself as emperor. These policies encouraged nationalism directly, and also indirectly through awakening national opposition to what was seen no longer as liberation but as French imperialism.

In the immediate post-Napoleonic period international society was in a curious state, being partly dynastic in character (Habsburg, Romanov and Hohenzollern) and partly nationalistic (Britain and France). It was this contradiction which aborted the attempt by Alexander I to create an inter-dynastic community of Europe and brought to an end the attempt at international government through Congresses. Not until the third quarter of the nineteenth century did the nationalisms which had been suppressed by the dynastic order of Metternich at last come into their own, and from then on the states-system of Europe changes in character. The dynasties either absorbed and utilised the new, emergent nationalisms – as did Prussia pan-Germanism, and Russia pan-Slavism – or were broken by them, as, eventually, was the Habsburg Monarchy.

Some political philosophers, as Richard Price and Thomas Paine before the French Revolution, and notably Mazzini after it, ascribed international conflict to dynastic rivalries, and held that the triumph of nationalism would inaugurate an era of international harmony.[4] Events were to prove them wrong, and it remains to ask why an international society based on nationalism should prove to be even more volatile than an international society founded on dynasticism.

In the first place the tension between state nation and culture nation has not been resolved, nor is it likely to be. A redrawing of state boundaries to correspond with linguistic boundaries – to say nothing of religious or racial ones – would produce a nightmare situation, with, for example, the political map of sub-Saharan Africa resembling a confetti continent. Yet while cultural nationalism exists, there will be pressure to change boundaries.

Conversely, while state nationalism not simply exists, but deems it its task to integrate the state on the basis of a homogeneous nation, there will be pressure culturally to conform. This is an element in the 'nation-building' task which many new states have set themselves and is a symptom of their sense of insecurity. The result will be a policy of 'cultural imperialism' against minorities such as has occurred in Kurdistan and the southern Sudan; the mass expulsion or fleeing of minorities as in the cases of the Palestinians, the Ugandan Asians and the Pieds Noirs; or even, in extreme instances, the mass murder of minorities as has been the fate of the Armenians and the German Jews. The refugee problem and the incidence of genocide are both features of nationalistic policies taken to their logical extremes.

Moreover, nationalism may lead not only to an exacerbation of conflict within states, but also between them. It arouses, or has the power to arouse, chauvinistic populist passions. It turns territory that to the dynast would be expendable into 'sacred' territory, and so produces an unprecedented resistance to peaceful change. The Palestine and Kashmir problems are but two that are totally insoluble in consequence. Finally, by transferring power, but not responsibility, to the mass of people, it will tend to encourage a greater recklessness in the handling of interstate relations than when power and responsibility are combined. 'They are ringing the bells', said Walpole when forced into war with Spain in 1739, 'they will soon be wringing their hands.' Lord Aberdeen in 1854, Napoleon III in July 1870, might well have echoed him.

The period from 1870 to 1914 was one of unparalleled nationalism in the states-system, and it gave to the diplomatic history of that era, and to the war which followed it, their peculiar character. The war, once started, could not be stopped, and the peace, given the passions aroused and the losses endured, could only be a punitive one. Since those times international society has been extended to encompass non-

Western states whose emancipation has usually been achieved through the growth of indigenous nationalist movements. Has the new nationalism the same potentiality for mischief as the old?

If it has not, the reason may lie less in the character of Third World nationalism than in the chronic economic and military weakness to which these new states are prone. But in one direction at least there would appear to be a marked difference. The embattled, hubristic nationalisms of the late nineteenth century existed in a self-contained world; they had nothing to fear but each other. The new states are still very much in the shadow of those nationalisms as manifested in the rival and rapacious imperialisms of the European powers. Having painfully achieved their freedom they are in no mood to lose it again, and unless in a position of political or economic desperation, tend to close ranks whenever an external or internal threat appears. Although nationalism has given the new states legitimacy, it is noteworthy that nationalist movements which have been denied statehood seldom receive any support from Third World states even when one might expect the pull of ethnic or religious ties. Thus neither Biafra nor the southern Sudan received any effective help from other African states.

III

There is thus a natural community of interest amongst the states of the Third World, or at least amongst continental or comparable groupings of such states. But can there be in international society as a whole? Can governments in a nationalistic age establish the community of interest that once characterised the society of princes?

There have been examples of this in the past. The Concert of Europe might be cited as one such, its *ad hoc* accommodations and arrangements being designed to safeguard the system and the reasonable interests of its members. The League of Nations was a more self-conscious attempt, for its architects desired that it should be set up on the principle of democratic nationalism, it having been conveniently ignored that democratic nationalism had largely produced the mood leading to the war. That the League was dominated by fairly satisfied Great Powers, and for the rest made up of small ones which had everthing to gain, and nothing to lose, from taking part, gave the international system prior to the upheavals of the 1930s a reputation for order and reason. But this had nothing to do with a community spirit derived from nationalism and was in any case illusory. And nothing that has occurred since then gives any grounds for hope that nationalism – at any rate nationalism harnessed to power and interest – can conceive of a community greater than itself.

It is this which differentiates the nation from, say, the regiment.

Regimental pride may admit of no rival in tradition, fighting quality and worth, but these attitudes in no way impair the efficiency or cohesiveness of the army; indeed this self-regarding spirit will make of the army a more vital and effective force. The difference, of course, is that in an army there is an underlying and ultimate loyalty to nation, sovereign, or cause, which subsumes the loyalty inspired by, and that required of, the regiment.

International society as a whole has been unable to find a cause of enough emotional appeal, or an enemy sufficiently alarming, to turn itself into a real community on a world scale. And short of a threat from outer space, or some global ecological disaster endangering all, it is difficult to see how it could. Even causes of oecumenical pretensions and, so their adherents would claim, universal validity, seem unable to hold their own against the centrifugal pull of nationalism. Thus the great unifying philosophy of Marxist-Leninism has been riven into orthodoxy and heresy (or heresy and orthodoxy) by the old nationalistic rivalry of Russia and China. The class enemy fades into history and so loses its efficacy as a political catalyst; the historical and national enemy, on the other hand, continually emphasised by a creed which makes of the nation a point of reference transcending time, is an enduring and provocative fact.

It is, however, possible that the world's rulers, at least, will discover for themselves a community of interest that is superficially like that of the princes in times past. However varied their cultural origins may be, they enjoy, for the most part, a similar life style, acquire similar tastes, cultivate transnational friendships and share in common – much more than their princely predecessors – the risks and dangers of political life in a violent and unstable world. They are therefore placed in a situation akin to that of legislators, developing 'horizontal' loyalties and affiliations – the House of Commons, it is claimed, is 'the best club in the world' – but mindful that their existence depends ultimately upon 'vertical' links with their 'constituencies', the nations. Thus although these shared interests and fears may result in a seeming community among the states themselves, there is the always present danger that this will be shattered by alienated nationalism, as the comparative harmony of the Locarno period was shattered by the emergence at state level of a virulent new nationalism from Germany.

IV

Whatever may be the problems and divisions of the political world, the view has often been expressed that in the economic realm an international community of interest might be developed from which political harmony, even unity, would ultimately come. This is, indeed, the idea which underlay the setting up of the European Economic Community. That such an idea could be realised on a world scale, or at any rate for the non-Communist world, is scarcely possible given the disparity of resources and of development that would need to be overcome. The hopes of Cobden and his school for a world made prosperous and peaceful by free trade have receded as the twentieth century has advanced. In truth the whole notion was a liberal fallacy, based on the premise that what was good for Manchester was likewise good for Madagascar. Much of modern nationalism has been a reaction to this doctrine. It has set out to recover the 'national soul' by evoking a rural or religious tradition, as have, in their various ways, De Valera, Gandhi and the Ayatollah Khomeini; or it has upheld the martial in contrast to the material virtues, as in the various forms of nationalistic fascism. But even without such reactions, only if there were permitted a free movement of peoples into the richer countries would the Cobdenite philosophy ensure not simply prosperity, but also a measure of economic justice, and even then the justice would be for individuals rather than for nations.

The nations, for their part, have increasingly taken their economic resources and activities into their own hands, and, if new and vulnerable, have largely done so out of a fear of exploitation. True, nationalism, despite the three examples just given, usually means development, a desire to be part of the modern world, even a contempt for tribal and traditional ways; yet in much Third World nationalism there also runs a strain of anti-Western resentment and suspicion, giving rise to fear of the return of foreign control exercised more subtly than before, and leading, often enough, to strict state regulation applied through a stifling bureaucracy. Moreover, in a time of recession all the pressures are towards economic nationalism rather than inter-nationalism: the reduction of aid; an ending, except for the professionally qualified, to the migration of labour; and the pressing of economic advantage, whether of resources, as with OPEC, or of exports, as with the Japanese, to a degree which has seriously threatened the viability of the whole system – a system, furthermore, now lacking the overall direction and stability which at one time Britain, and more recently the United States, provided. Even the members of the European Community have tended to resist the centralising tendencies to which they are subject, and such has been the working out of the Common Agricultural Policy, together with a more general disenchantment, that the continuance of Britain's membership is even now not wholly free from doubt. Clearly, much of recent national sentiment has become suspicious and critical of further economic integration unless the advantages are manifest. Nor is this all. For nationalism, by impelling many poor countries out of pride to go for high, rather than for intermediate or basic, technology, or our of fear to shoulder defence burdens which they are least able to bear, as well as by producing, all too frequently, the unsettled conditions which discourage investment, is more likely to have accentuated than to have ameliorated the inequalities and strains in the world economic order.

V

A world political community, or a world economic community out of which the former might emerge, looks, therefore, at least in present conditions, unrealisable. Some might hold that the United Nations is a living embodiment of the political, but it is, in truth, but the shell of a dead international community, the wartime alliance, in which, as it were, other creatures have come to live. Yet states have succeeded in forming communities of interest, either political, strategical, economic, or to fulfil some other function, and often on a regional basis. But in such cases nationalism has usually been less the motive force than something to be circumvented, as with Greece and Turkey in NATO, reconciled, as with France and Germany in the postwar co-operation culminating in the EEC, or utilised and exploited in such Third World bodies as the Arab League and the Organisation of African Unity. The unhappy histories of these last two, as well as of most 'pan-national' movements, illustrate how difficult it seems to be for nationalism to sink its own identity in a greater cause.

Yet it is the possibility, attractiveness, or necessity of creating a greater than national community out of not simply interest, but emotional identification, which has often preoccupied governments and fired the imagination of idealists. States, of course, as abstract or posited beings, cannot have emotions. People alone can have emotions; but if a state's population can be made to feel a certain way this may well bear upon that state's relations with others. In every alliance, therefore, the propaganda agencies seek to create an emotional bond with the allies, and then a feeling of family is a side of the Commonwealth relationship which, although indubitably less strong than when the dominions followed the mother country into war, is still deemed sufficiently important constantly to be given royal encouragement.

A community founded on interest with the support or disguise of emotion is one thing, but can there be a community of sentiment alone, a bond, amongst nations, of sympathy, understanding, affection, in short, 'fraternity'?

The idea of a brotherhood of nations arose in the late eighteenth century. Anthony Smith, who describes this as polycentric nationalism, has not detected any previous instance of it.[5] Probably the earlier association of the nation with religion, and religion claiming to have a monopoly of truth, rendered any wider sympathy impossible. Religious nationalism, whether of the ancient Jews, or of Cromwellian England, was essentially monocentric, and so developed a 'chosen people' ideology.[6] The idea that nations were of equal value was thus a product of the secularism, as belief in the brotherhood of all mankind was a feature of the romanticism, of the late eighteenth century. Schiller reflected these tendencies both in his *An die Freude* (Ode to Joy) and in his literary celebrations of the national struggles of the Dutch, the Swiss and the French. In a letter to a friend he wrote:

'We of the modern world are endowed with a realm of interest unknown to Greek and Roman alike. With it the patriotic spirit simply cannot compete. The latter is really significant only for immature peoples, the youth of the world . . . It is a poor and paltry idea to write for *one* nation.'[7]

Such sentiments were essentially those of a cosmopolitan counter-culture, that represented by the Byrons, Bolívars and Mazzinis of their day, as later by the Guevaras, Cohn-Bendits and Tariq Alis of our own. But the nationalism of idealistic dissent, appealing chiefly to youth and to the bourgeoisie, had neither the weight nor the staying power of nationalism harnessed to the power, wealth and interests of states. The apotheosis of nationalism came not only with its adaptation to the needs of the European Establishments, but with its almost complete triumph over the newly politicised working classes during the closing decades of the nineteenth century. In this way were the peoples of Europe for the first time firmly bound to the rivalries of their respective states, rivalries which emotionally they came fully to share. It was this which gave to the First World War its peculiarly absolute and horrific character.

VI

Yet despite all its failings, and in many ways its terrible history, nationalism is the great political 'cult' of much of the world today. It has given to many otherwise rootless people that sense of identity and belonging of which the break-up of feudalism, or the migration from country to town, had deprived them. It has been used to defend languages and cultures that are threatened by others, and to obtain or to safeguard homelands and frontiers. Above all it plays an essential role in the task of 'nation-building' in those states where nothing remotely like a nation had ever existed before. Despite all attacks upon it, and criticisms of it, the nation-state is still the most effective and efficient type of polity there is. And if states exist simply because Lord Salisbury or Delcassé once took a ruler and drew a frontier for a colony that has now become a state, then somehow or other the people living in that state have to be encouraged to think of themselves as a nation and to become conscious of the national idea. This is no easy task. Often the tribe, or the extended family, is the focus of maximum loyalty, and this has to be broken down if new attitudes are to flourish. It is the very lack of security, or cohesiveness, or self-confidence that makes the nationalism of some new states seem so exaggerated or flamboyant. Like adolescents anxious to demonstrate their adulthood, they become caricatures of what they are attempting to be.

Perhaps in this there lies some cause for optimism. It may be that as today, in the West, we read the naïve and theatrical speeches of Theodore Roosevelt and William II with astonishment, those in the Third World will one day look back with amused detachment at the rhetorical excesses of their own early nationalisms. A transient immaturity, however, is not, alas, the only feature of contemporary nationalism making difficult the development of a true spirit of international community. The malaise is deeper than that. Even if such a spirit were not to prove vulnerable to the disruptive dynamics of international politics, the *hubris*, intolerance and subjection of means to ends of some present-day nationalist movements would indicate a dire moral sickness in late twentieth-century international society. For in an age which has largely shed belief in a transcendent God, the deification of the nation has filled a void. And one's god, by definition, can do no wrong. The 'chosen people' myth may have encouraged ruthlessness and stubbornness in the ancient Jews, but at least they were capable of national repentance, of confessing the sins of the whole people in sackcloth and ashes. No such humility is a mark of modern extreme nationalist movements, for in their moral autonomy, and as moral automata given to nation-worship, they have succumbed to the sin of idolatry, capable only of creating with their antagonists a community of Hell.

Such a situation poses a profound challenge not only to enlightened statesmanship but also to enlightened citizenship. Only statesmanship can so recast the character of the state, remould its institutions, or redraw its boundaries, that the fundamental cause of minority or irredentist nationalism, an inability to identify with the state of residence, leading to severe or even total alienation, is removed or at least diminished. But enlightened citizenship may do something to lessen the injustice, intolerance, even ignorance and lack of interest, which have exacerbated such alienation. All this is much to require, both when historical conditioning ensures that enmities are ingrained and memories of ancient wrongs preserved, and when justice cannot be accorded to one side without its denial to the other. Yet so long as the problems remain unresolved, the traumas unassuaged, so long will the coexistence of nationalism and the spirit of international community be at best but a partial and a fragile achievement.

NOTES: CHAPTER 3

1 Ortega y Gassett, *The Revolt of the Masses* (London: Allen & Unwin, 1961), p. 124.
2 See Kurt Mendelssohn, FRS, *The Riddle of the Pyramids* (London: Thames & Hudson, 1974), p. 153. The prehistorian Aubrey Burl has speculated that a similar motive may have led to the construction of Silbury Hill: A. Burl, *Prehistoric Avebury* (New Haven, Conn.: Yale University Press, 1979), p. 136.
3 All three idealised patriotism and identified nation with people. Herder emphasised ethnicity by seeing the nation as organic and possessed of a unique *Volksgeist* expressed in language. Fichte stressed the need for political struggle to achieve national self-awareness.
4 See, for example: 'Richard Price's Journal', *The National Library of Wales Journal*, vol. XXI, no. 4 (Winter 1980), pp. 398–9; Thomas Paine, *The Rights of Man* (London: Dent, Everyman edn, 1963), p. 170; Mazzini, Letter to Ernst Haug, 1863, and extract from Autobiography, in N. Ganjulee (ed.), *Guiseppe Mazzini: Selected Writings* (London: Lindsay Drummond, 1945), pp. 118, 125–6. I am indebted to Dr D. O. Thomas, the editor of Price's Letters, for the first reference. Price is also interesting to the student of nationalism for following the older practice of taking the statist rather than the ethnic view of nationality. Although of Welsh birth, he always thought of himself as an Englishman, as did Swift, of Irish birth, earlier in the century. This has not endeared Price to Welsh nationalism although 'England' then meant the state, a usage still preserved on the continent.
5 Anthony D. Smith, *Theories of Nationalism* (London: Duckworth, 1971), pp. 160, 171. The most he has found are hints in a few classical writers.
6 See Milton on God's choice of 'His Englishmen' to achieve divine purposes: *Areopagitica*, in *Milton's Prose Writings* (London: Dent, Everyman edn, 1958), p. 177. The pan-Slav movement was also essentially a monocentric religious nationalism.
7 Letter of Schiller to Christian Gottfried Körner in *Friedrich Schiller: An Anthology for Our Time* (New York: Frederick Ungar, 1959), p. 20.

Part Two
The Conventional Morality of States

4

International Law

HIDEMI SUGANAMI

It is the purpose of this chapter to examine the links between the community of states and international law.

Does the operation of international law presuppose the idea of the community of states? What legal and behavioural characteristics can we expect a community of states to exhibit? If the community of states does not yet exist, can international law assist its coming into existence?

Before discussing these questions, however, it is necessary first to examine briefly the relationship between sovereignty and international law. For, whatever form the constellation of states may take, it is with reference to the constellation of *sovereign* states that this chapter attempts to analyse its possible links with the law of nations.

I

There is one complaint against international law which, but for its persistence, would not have to be taken too seriously. It is the claim that states cannot be bound (that is, obligated) by international law because they are 'sovereign'. One of the implications of this claim is that between sovereign states there can be no society or community.

This complaint against international law, however, is based on a semantic confusion as regards the word 'sovereignty'. This point has been repeatedly made by C. A. W. Manning, but I shall outline his contention here as it has not received the attention it deserves.

In presenting Manning's analysis of 'sovereignty', it is important to note that, instead of trying to identify the one true meaning of that word, he seeks to observe how that word is actually used in different contexts.

From this viewpoint, Manning notes that the word in question is used, first, in the discussion about who possesses 'sovereignty' within a particular state. Second, he notices that when the word is used in the context of determining what is to count as a sovereign state, it refers to a different concept. Third, when it is argued, for instance, that a certain state is going to lose part of its 'sovereignty' by becoming a party to some treaty, the word is being used to indicate yet another idea.[1]

The word 'sovereignty' in the first context may be interchangeable with a term such as 'the supreme political authority', and when used in the third context, it is equivalent to an expression such as 'the sum of residual legal freedom'. Manning does not explain in detail what the word means when used in the second context, but simply points out that it refers to 'an aspect of their [states'] nature as organizations constitutionally insular'.[2] It is his contention that what it 'means' to be a 'constitutionally insular' entity can be known only through a further investigation of the historically contingent institutional facts of international relations.[3]

It may be noted that Manning's sovereignty sense-number-one and sense-number-two are inseparable. The existence of sovereign authority within a political community and the fact that the political community is a sovereign state are two sides of the same coin: there cannot be one without the other, given the coexistence of sovereign states.

However, it is vital to stress that sovereignty sense-number-one is a predicate of a political body (the government, or those who rule) within a state and that sovereignty sense-number-two is a predicate of the state as such. It is therefore misleading to say that sovereignty has internal and external *aspects*. The subject of the 'internal' sovereignty and that of the 'external' sovereignty are two different things: one the government (or those who rule in the name of the state), the other the personified entity behind it, the state.

As regards the argument that states cannot be bound by international law because they are 'sovereign', it must be noted that there is nothing inherent in the meaning of the word 'sovereign' in this context, that is, 'constitutionally insular', that logically contradicts the ability of 'sovereign' states to have obligations towards one another. And it is one of the historically contingent institutional facts of contemporary international relations that international law is capable of creating obligations for 'constitutionally insular' political communities. Thus the argument in question must be rejected in so far as it purports to be a statement of fact about the institutional structure of contemporary international relations.

It is possible, however, that someone who maintains that states, being 'sovereign', cannot be bound by international law does not mean to make a statement of fact, but is advancing a normative assertion to the effect that states, being 'sovereign', need not fulfil obligations emanating from international law.

It is perfectly reasonable to hold that there may be some circumstances in which states need not obey international law. The contrary thesis, that is, that international law must always be obeyed, is very difficult to sustain. But it is absurd to suggest that the nature of states as 'organizations constitutionally insular' can as such be taken as the reason for unconditionally rejecting the necessity to obey any part of international law whatsoever.

In fact, those who argue that states, being 'sovereign', need not obey international law appear to regard the word 'sovereign' (here used as a noun) as having only one true meaning, that is, the person, real or notional, who is not subject to law and whose will we must always obey. If this is the only true meaning of the word, and if states are identified as 'sovereign' (here used as an adjective), then it naturally follows that states, being 'sovereign', need not obey international law.

However, those who uphold such a line of argument must show: (1) why the word 'sovereign' must be regarded as having only one true meaning; (2) why its meaning is what they claim it to be; and (3) why states, that is, 'constitutionally insular' political communities, should automatically be regarded as 'sovereign' in that sense.

None of these questions can be given a satisfactory answer. Consequently, the argument that there can be no society or community of sovereign states must be rejected in so far as the argument is based on the idea that sovereign states cannot be bound by international law.

II

It has been noted that it is one of the institutional facts of contemporary international relations that international law is capable of creating obligations for sovereign states. But beyond this observation, one can ask a further question: is it necessary for those who act and talk in the name of states to assume that states form a 'community' in order that they can operate international law? If the idea of 'community' is unnecessary, is it still possible to say that the idea of 'society' or 'system' of states is a logical precondition for the operation of international law? There are two approaches to this question.

It is, on the one hand, possible to deny the meaning of the question by arguing that the idea of international law operating among states is part of the definitions of 'international system', 'society' and 'community'. It may, for instance, be suggested that these are constellations of states in which different types of international law operate (see section III), or that these are to be differentiated in terms of the degree of the effectiveness of international law.

If such an approach is accepted, then it becomes meaningless to ask whether the idea of 'international system', 'society', or 'community' is presupposed by '(the operation of) international law' for this will then be regarded as being conceptually integral to all of them.

It may, on the other hand, be argued that 'international system', 'society', or 'community' need not be defined in terms of law. Manning appears to take this position as regards 'society', which he seems to use as a general term, and not, at any rate, explicitly in contradistinction to 'system' or 'community'. In his view, a 'society' is a body of individuals who share a set of basic assumptions about themselves, of which the most fundamental is the idea that they are 'persons' forming a 'society'. Similarly, in Manning's view, there is an 'international society' in the sense that those who act and talk in the name of states regard sovereign states as 'persons' forming their own 'society'.

Manning insists that 'personality' and 'subjection to law', that is, 'legal personality', are not identical and that the former is logically prior to the latter.[4] Thus, in his view, the idea that sovereign states are 'persons' forming a 'society' is a logical precondition for the operation of international law.[5]

It is not entirely clear what is meant by 'society' in this context, for 'law', its usual ingredient, has been deliberately left out. But we may assume that the idea of 'states as "persons" forming a "society"' entails a cluster of basic principles, for example, that they ought to live in harmony with one another, or reciprocate one another, that they ought to treat one another as equals in status, and so on. Unless these principles have been accepted by states, it may be argued, international law cannot operate.

But the state of affairs in which a set of states accept these basic principles need not be paraphrased in sociological terms at all. And if we wish to do so, a general term, 'a society of states', seems sufficient. There seems no need to call in the idea of 'community', distinguished in some way from that of 'society', and to say that the state of affairs ought really to be labelled a 'community'.

On the assumption that 'system', 'society' and 'community' signify an ascending order of willingness to co-operate, it may be suggested that international law functions most effectively when international relations are conducted on the belief that states form a 'community'. But the 'most effective functioning' of international law naturally presupposes that international law is already in operation. Thus the idea of the 'community of states' held by the practitioners of international relations cannot be said to be a logical precondition for the operation of international law.

III

It may be assumed that 'system', 'society' and 'community' signify an ascending order of social solidarity. But how can we assess the degree of social solidarity between states? And what can we expect a 'community of states' to look like? These questions must be dealt with before we can examine the third question noted at the outset: if the community of states does not yet exist, can international law assist its coming into existence?

One way of assessing the degree of social solidarity between states is to look at the type of international law which is accepted by them. This can be done at least in two ways.

First, we may take as the criterion the degree of centralisation in the law that binds states. This can be expected to be closely linked with the degree of social solidarity (consensus and co-operation) among them for, unless states have achieved a high degree of consensus, they are unlikely to agree to be bound by a highly centralised legal system. Conversely, a higher degree of co-operation may be facilitated by a higher degree of centralisation in the law.

From such a viewpoint, we may argue that a 'community of states' must be legally more highly centralised than a 'society of states', and that this more so than a 'system of states'. This way of ordering the three terms appears to be in line with common parlance. For we use the expression 'European Community' to refer to the most highly centralised union of states in the contemporary world. The League of Nations, which was considerably less centralised, was called the 'Société des Nations'. And the word 'Staatensystem' was popularly used to refer to the even less centralised (balance-of-power) structure by the writers of the Napoleonic period.[6]

Using these historical cases as paradigms, we may take the existence of a supranational organisation as a sufficient condition for 'community', that of an international organisation as a sufficient condition for 'society' and the absence of any special organs as a ground for regarding the relevant set of states as forming only a 'system'. It does not follow, however, that to deserve the label 'community', states must have supranational organs, or that, to be entitled to be called a 'society', they must be equipped with some special international organs. It will be artificial to treat these terms as rigidly definable categories.

In using international law as an indicator of social solidarity among states, however, we may focus our attention not on the degree of centralisation, but on the character of the subject-matter covered by the law.

Here classifications offered by Georg Schwarzenberger, Wolfgang Friedmann and Stanley Hoffmann are useful. These writers are not agreed on terminology, but their substantive contentions are close enough to justify an attempt at summarising their classifications in one scheme.

Contemporary international law may thus be said to encompass two types: law that sets out the minimum conditions for the coexistence of states and law that facilitates a higher degree of co-operation among them.

Among the first type may be included general international law principles of effectiveness, *pacta sunt servanda, pacta tertiis nec nocent nec prosunt,* self-defence, reprisals, non-intervention, freedom of the high seas, laws of war and neutrality, as well as treaties determining the territorial boundaries of particular states.

Among the second type are a number of treaties for a higher degree of co-operation in the economic sphere, laws pertaining to scientific and technological collaboration, and to environmental issues, social welfare and humanitarian ideals.

Between these two types, there is law regulating common international problems such as the status of diplomats, settlement of disputes, treaty-making, extraditions, commerce and transport.

The first type of law may be termed the law of coexistence, the second type the law of co-operation and the intermediate type the law of co-ordination. While the distinction between the first two types is relatively clear, the difference between the neighbouring two types is somewhat blurred.[7]

It has been pointed out by Hedley Bull that the progress from the law of coexistence to the law of co-operation does not necessarily show that the former has become more firmly established because the latter has been able to build on it.[8] But it seems more to the point to say that a systematic development of the law of co-operation can hardly be expected to take place among a set of states if they are still at the stage where their interactions require effective regulation most urgently in terms of the law of coexistence – where, for instance, the violation of treaties, use of force and territorial disputes are the order of the day.

Thus, if one assumes that 'system', 'society' and 'community' signify an ascending order of social solidarity, and that, as the level of social solidarity heightens, the purpose to which regulation by international law is vitally relevant shifts from 'co-existence' to 'co-operation', it will not be unreasonable to suggest that the law of coexistence indicates the existence of the 'system of states', that the law of co-ordination combined with the law of coexistence denotes the existence of the 'society of states', and that the expansion of the law of co-operation implies the coming-into-existence of the 'community of states'.

Whether one takes as the relevant criterion the degree of centralisation in the law or the character of the subject-matter covered by it, one reaches a roughly similar conclusion as regards the quality of contemporary international relations. It is that there have been attempts at transforming what was essentially a 'system of states' into a 'society' at the global level, that these attempts have been successful to a considerable degree in many fields, although in some regions or between some states (for example, in the Middle East) the element of 'system' is perhaps more pronounced, and that most notably in Western Europe there have been serious attempts at creating a 'community'.

However, one important qualification must be made as regards the attempt to determine the degree of social solidarity between states in terms of the types of international law accepted by them. It is the very obvious fact that actual policies pursued by states are not necessarily in conformity with their legal commitments. The language of the Treaty of Rome, for instance, cannot be taken by itself to suggest that its members constitute a 'community' in real terms. A content-analysis and a classification of international legal commitments provide only a rough, though indispensable, indicator of the degree of unity among the separate sovereign states.

Thus, there is a need to work out, however tentatively, what a 'community of states' is expected to look like, not in terms of the types of international law, but in terms of behavioural and attitudinal characteristics of states. On the assumption that a 'community of states' exhibits a very high degree of social solidarity, we may venture to suggest that, for a set of states to form a 'community':

(1) They must not be actively engaged in territorial disputes among themselves. Any such dispute ought to have been resolved, settled, or have ceased to be an important issue among them.

(2) Use or threat of force must be practically unthinkable among them, and they must share readiness for peaceful change and settlement of disputes in their relationships.

(3) They must be satisfied that law regulating their relationships is broadly acceptable and is generally being observed.

(4) There must be substantial movement of goods, persons and ideas across the frontiers with a minimum of restrictions.

(5) They must be engaged in a joint effort to secure a minimum standard of welfare.

(6) They must be committed to co-operate in future.

The first three criteria demand that the states enjoy a very high degree of order in their mutual intercourse. But orderly relationships could be maintained between states even if they kept the level of intercourse relatively low. Such a set of states could not be regarded as a 'community of states', for 'community' implies a substantial amount of intercourse among its members. Thus the fourth criterion has been added, which demands that the movement of goods, persons and ideas must be substantial. It also demands that restrictions on the freedom of movement across the borders be kept to a minimum, for such restrictions are likely to be contrary to the idea of a 'community'.

The fifth criterion suggests that a low standard in one country must be regarded as a common concern of all the others. And the sixth criterion demands that the states must be committed to continue to live as members of the community. This suggests that the peoples of the member-states must share a sense not only of common interest but common destiny, without which a community will not be viable.

This is a very demanding set of criteria, but if they are fully satisfied, it can hardly be disputed that the states concerned form a 'community', and not merely a 'system' or a 'society'. A constellation of states that does not satisfy these criteria fully may still be regarded as forming a 'community', but the further it departs from them, the less 'community-like' it becomes.

If such a set of criteria is accepted as a defining condition of a true 'community of states', it is clear that states do not form a 'community' at the global level in contemporary international relations, although between some states, the idea of a 'community' has been considered as a possible goal for the future. The question remains as to whether international law can assist the coming-into-existence of a 'community of states'.

IV

It is clear that the development of a 'system' or 'society' of states into a 'community' as characterised by the set of behavioural or attitudinal features spelled out above is inconceivable without some assistance of international law.

In the first place, a machinery for regular intergovernmental consultation, and some form of international court of justice or arbitration will be necessary to sustain the very high degree of order expected in their mutual intercourse. Moreover, a substantial movement of goods, persons and ideas across the frontiers with a minimum of restrictions require agreement and regulation by treaties. A joint effort to prevent the standard of welfare of each nation from falling below a minimum requires international law to declare where the minimum standard lies (for example, a declaration of human rights) and to establish some institutional device to co-ordinate their effort. And commitment to future co-operation is expressed and consolidated by the enshrinement of their corporate will in some basic treaties.

In fact it is inconceivable for any set of states to exhibit the degree of co-operation which is expected of a 'community of states' unless the system of law that governs it is relatively centralised and contains in it a substantial amount of what was earlier called the 'law of co-operation'. As a corollary, it might be thought that a relatively centralised system of international law containing a substantial amount of the 'law of co-operation' was, once accepted, capable of driving a constellation of states towards a real 'community' even if initially the effectiveness of the law was limited. At any rate, it might be argued that unless some progress in the law has been made, a 'society of states' could never develop into a 'community'. This line of argument is typically an idealist position, but finds support among a wider spectrum of writers.[9]

However, two points need to be noted. First, for a progress in the law to be possible there must be sufficient initial support, among the relevant governments and peoples, for any such progress. And such support is unlikely unless the relationships between the states concerned are already reasonably orderly. Second, it should be clear that, for international law, which has been accepted, to be capable of moulding the course of history in the direction it aims at, the participants must share a long-term orientation towards the eventual implementation of their legal commitments and aspirations. The extent to which such an attitude can be cultivated in one state depends not so much on the aspirations enshrined in the law themselves as on the willingness of the other states to progress in the same direction. Moreover, because aspirations and commitments enshrined in the law are likely to be open to contending interpretations, depending on one's value-preferences, the willingness of the states to progress in the *same* direction presupposes a broad consensus among them on the issues of value.[10] Thus although international law is indispensable for the creation of the 'community of states', this cannot be brought into existence where there is no concurrence of national wills' to work towards unity. Some critics of idealism go further and assert that international law must not aspire to what states cannot realistically be expected to achieve, and that the twentieth-century trend in international law is already harmfully progressivist in some areas.[11]

How the concurrence of national wills towards unity can come about is a question that goes beyond the scope of this chapter. But it may well be that this is possible only where there is a common history of suffering: through this, nations may be encouraged to look into the future with a sense of common destiny, without which the 'community of states' will remain an idea without a secure foundation. Whether the heightened awareness of what Richard Falk has called the 'endangered planet', that is, common suffering in anticipation, is capable of producing the concurrence of national wills remains to be seen.[12]

It might be suggested that the concurrence of national wills towards unity could come about partly through the propagation of the idea that states were to be regarded as forming a 'community' rather than merely a 'society' or 'system'. But it seems that for states, in any serious sense, to regard one another as forming a 'community' *is* to have the concurrence of national wills towards unity. The crucial question is how it is possible to make states begin seriously to regard themselves as forming a 'community', and this cannot be answered by saying that they must. This problem of transition remains one of the most important tasks for the theory of international law and relations.[13]

NOTES: CHAPTER 4

1 C. A. W. Manning, 'The legal framework in a world of change', in *The Aberystwyth Papers: International Politics 1919–1969*, ed. B. Porter (London: Oxford University Press, 1972), p. 308.
2 ibid., p. 307.
3 C. A. W. Manning, *The Nature of International Society*, reissue (London: Macmillan, 1975), p. 103.
4 ibid., p. 24.
5 ibid., p. x.
6 Hedley Bull, *The Anarchical Society: A Study of Order in World Politics* (London: Macmillan, 1977), p. 12.
7 Georg Schwarzenberger, *A Manual of International Law*, 5th edn (London: Stevens, 1967), pp. 10–15; Wolfgang Friedmann, *The Changing Structure of International Law* (London: Stevens, 1964), pp. 65–7; Stanley Hoffmann, *The State of War: Essays on the Theory and Practice of International Politics* (London: Praeger, 1965), pp. 97–8.
8 Bull, op. cit., p. 153.
9 A good illustration of idealism is to be found in Sir Hersch Lauterpacht, *The Function of Law in the International Community* (Oxford: Clarendon Press, 1933). See also K. Deutsch, 'The probability of international law', in *The Relevance of International Law: A Festschrift for Professor Leo Gross*, ed. Karl Deutsch and Stanley Hoffmann (Cambridge, Mass.: Schenkman, 1968), esp. p. 83.
10 Thus both legalistic idealism of Lauterpacht and non-legalistic policy-orientated approach of Myres MacDougal have serious weaknesses. For the latter, see Richard Falk, *The Status of Law in International Society* (Princeton, NJ: Princeton University Press, 1970), p. 14.
11 See Hedley Bull, 'The Grotian conception of international society', in *Diplomatic Investigations: Essays in the Theory of International Politics*, ed. Herbert Butterfield and Martin Wight (London: Allen & Unwin, 1966).
12 See Richard Falk, *This Endangered Planet: Prospects and Proposals for Human Survival* (New York: Vintage Books, 1971).
13 See Richard Falk, 'A new paradigm for international legal studies: prospects and proposals', *The Yale Law Journal*, vol. 84, no. 5 (April 1975), pp. 969–1021, but also J. S. Watson, 'A realistic jurisprudence of international law', in *The Year Book of World Affairs 1980* (London: Stevens, 1980), pp. 265–85.

5
Realpolitik

JOHN VINCENT

Six hours before he died, Bismarck is said to have raised his hand sharply and cried: 'That is impossible on grounds of general public policy.'[1] It is interesting that the modern founder of the model of a dynamic foreign policy should, at the end, have invoked reason of state against rather than for something. But inaction as well as action can form the basis of an 'operational philosophy', by which I mean one which informs the actual conduct of world politics as distinct from merely rearranging reality according to the preferences of this or that school of utopian thought. Realism rather than utopianism is what distinguishes the philosophy that is the concern of this chapter. It is now most often called 'power politics', though the nineteenth-century expression '*Realpolitik*', and the seventeenth-century one '*raison d'état*' still survive. It is true that none of these phrases are central to the contemporary idiom as sketched in Chapter 1, concerned as it is with equality, nationalism and modernisation. This may simply be a matter of fashion. Or it may be that *Realpolitik* has lost its force as an operational philosophy. Or, to the contrary, it may remain a grisly reality to which our attention need hardly be drawn. These are questions on which this chapter must attempt to conclude. In any event, the intention is to proceed by way of an exposition of the doctrine of *Realpolitik*, to a search for its place in contemporary international politics, and thence to a view of its relation to the idea of world community. What marks off this endeavour from the pursuit of a Community of Mankind[2] is the idea of a common interest rather than that of a common good.

I

The retention of the expression *Realpolitik* in the title of this chapter, and the extensive reference to *raison d'état* in the paragraphs which follow, will not one hopes be taken as the mannered antiquarianism of someone who has failed to come to terms with the twentieth century. They are retained because they have a particularly operational ring as names for philosophies worked out at the bar of practice, as well as enjoying a position in the categories of the scholars. The distinction between *raison d'état* and *Realpolitik* is not, for the present purpose, an important one. There might be more blood and iron about the second, more subtlety and cunning about the first, but they have in common three characteristics which provide a structure for this passage of the argument. There is, first, the preoccupation with the state as the datum of world politics: by definition in the case of *raison d'état*; in the case of *Realpolitik* by its tendency to celebrate the state as the highest human achievement. Secondly, politics are power politics whether one likes it or not, and there is the recognition even in *Realpolitik* that some do not. Thirdly, the inevitability of power politics does not reduce politics to mere arbitrariness: the politics of power are a construction of humanity not an abandonment of it, and in this enterprise reason has had its part.

The centrality of the state in the theory we are considering has its origin in the policy of Richelieu, both domestic and foreign. It has been suggested that it was in the building of the French state in the seventeenth century that the doctrine of *raison d'état* was worked out, so that practice informed theory and theory practice.[3] Reason of state was the justification of central authority against mighty subjects, against religious dissidents as well as the established church, and even against the king himself as Richelieu taught Louis XIII that to act for the state he might sometimes have to violate ordinary morality.[4] In foreign policy, reason of state was the justification for departure from solidarity with co-religionists in international affairs, so that France could align herself against the Habsburgs rather than with them. Both these strands of policy contributed to the idea of the good of the state which was to be determined not according to religious categories, but according to those of reason. We shall see later that this doctrine of the autonomy of the state became, in German theory, one of primacy, blotting out any more inclusive notion of political attachment.

The second characteristic of the theory of *Realpolitik* under scrutiny here was that of international politics as the politics of power, like it or not. Under this head the question is raised of the relationship between politics and morality. The exponents of realism have power and morality working together within the state, but not in international relations where no overriding power exists to uphold a universal morality. In some versions of the theory of *Realpolitik*, this absence of a universal morality is taken to mean also the absence of any morality, so that Bismarck's advocacy of a Prussian attack on Austria is advanced 'for no other reason than the auspicious moment'.[5] In other versions, there is regret that morality must take second place to power as in that particular tradition of *raison d'état* which Meinecke depicts as a course followed in consciousness of its sinfulness.[6] In a third version of the theory of *Realpolitik* this consciousness of sin is rationalised in the doctrine of a double morality, a public and a private morality sharply distinguished, with state policy requiring the victory of the former. 'The statesman has no right', said Treitschke, 'to warm his hands with smug self-laudation at the smoking ruins of his fatherland, and comfort himself by saying "I have never lied".'[7]

It was the defence of the fatherland that made private morality possible, and this was Richelieu's defence of *raison d'état*. Certainly it might require that ordinary principles of morality be set aside, but this was service to a higher morality not its negation. Attention to the interests of the state provided the order within which the church might flourish. There was not a tension, as his zealous opponents argued, between service to the church and service to the state. It was not only possible, but also right, to be a 'Catholic of State'.[8] Bismarck echoed this when he said: 'I believe that I am obeying God when I serve the king.'[9]

The difficulty with doctrines of this kind which comfortably associated right with power is how God or Reason actually get into the act, as distinct from being forced to applaud at its conclusion. This is the problem for our third aspect of *raison d'état*, which insists on reason of state and not on whim, or power, or any other arbitrariness. One solution, spectacular but unhelpful, has been to describe *raison d'état* as 'the State's first law of Motion'.[10] From this attempt to assimilate politics to the natural sciences derives the doctrine of necessity, the idea that states cannot do otherwise than adhere to the precepts of *raison d'état* and the doctrine of interests laying down for each state the railway lines along which it should run. All that can emerge from this source is the baleful pronouncement that history could not have been other than it was because the states which made it were following the rule-book written for them in nature. Richelieu's notion of reason as 'the rule of conduct for a state'[11] is less deterministic. It allows for choice among purposes, and among means to those ends, decreeing only that reason and not another thing should be the instrument with which the choice of policy should be made. But from the point of view of operational philosophy, this doctrine of reason for states is hardly more helpful than the pseudo-science of reason of states: the latter is empty, the former full of the preferences, however reasonable, of the filler.

No doubt it would be possible to put together a list of maxims that might illustrate the prescriptive element in *raison d'état*: 'make of your enemy's enemy your friend'; 'take care in this war lest you be weakened for the next'; 'intervene only when there is a prospect of a successful outcome'; and so forth. If maxims of this kind have any moral content at all it is provided by the attention they pay to the virtue of prudence. The primacy of interest in the doctrine of *raison d'état* does not exclude the possibility that right conduct and interested behaviour might coincide.[12] Nor is this solely the doctrine of students of international relations corrupted by the material they have become too accustomed to handling. Professor R. M. Hare has cast doubt on the distinction between morality and expediency. 'Both morality and expediency', he writes, 'are matters of considering the consequences of the actions between which we have to choose, and choosing that action, which has the consequences which we think, in the circumstances, we ought to bring about.'[13] He goes on to say that the thing that morality adds to *interest*, and to *self*, is a calculation of consequences that would be chosen by anybody.

The difficulty with this defence of reason of state is that it is a doctrine that remains in the hands of somebody and not of anybody. And the unkind conclusion to this treatment of the theory of *Realpolitik* might be that it is an unhelpful prescription for state behaviour, that it is morally flawed by having only an accidental connection between interests and right, and that this being so it has no hold over the unscrupulous. Against this might be said that in the modern history of Europe the doctrine of *raison d'état* was clear enough to help establish the claims of the state against rival claimants to authority, that its insistence on reason of *state* meant that even the sovereign was subject to a discipline beyond himself, and that the requirement of *reason* of state provided that politics in a secular age would not be at sea without rudder or compass. In all this *raison d'état* and *Realpolitik* were undeniably operational philosophies: the justifications of the statesmen themselves, or of the publicists they promoted, which then instructed the deliberations of the scholars.

Whatever its historical function, the theory of power politics seems not to open a promising route to the establishment or even the conception of a world community. The tendency of the theorists of *Realpolitik* would be to treat the universalist conceptions of right, entailed in the notion of a world community, as a species of imperialism, seeking to make general the values of a mere part within the whole. And the parts are indissoluble if as states they are the 'most important and vital of historical forms'[14] providing the only possible arena for the realisation of human perfection. The only notion of world community which the theory of *Realpolitik* seems to allow is that of the culture of the world embodied in states collected together in a global pageant whose richness is dependent on the preservation of their separateness. Moreover, this is not the same world community as that, say, of the German romantic nationalist writers like Herder, who also believed in a global pageant, because in it there is an expectation more of conflict than of harmony.

The idea of international society is not so emasculated by the doctrine of *Realpolitik* as is that of world community. Society, as I shall suggest at greater length in the last section of this chapter, is a less demanding arrangement than community requiring merely the overlap of separate interests and not a unity of sentiment or of principle. The cautious pursuit of interests might be rendered as prudence and the function that this virtue might fulfil in restraining the behaviour of states was remarked above. The related idea of *convenance*, suggesting not merely what is convenient, but also what is conventional, was set forth in the eighteenth century as an underpinning of the European system in the absence of feudal or dynastic ties.[15] In this doctrine, the ideas of Europe as a whole, and of a European balance were not excluded by the sacred egotism of the state. Indeed, in the classical theory of the balance of powers, the independence of the parts of the system came to be dependent on equilibrium in the system as a whole. Thus *raison d'état* was stretched into reason of states, and each participant in the system was to recognise the limitations on its behaviour which the system itself imposed. The sections that follow will seek the place of doctrines of *Realpolitik* in contemporary world politics, and ask whether contemporary circumstances, which are not the same as those that accompanied the emergence of the classical theory, are not more hospitable to a connection between *Realpolitik* and world community.

II

A popular American distinction divides the tribe of international relationists into traditionalists and modernists.[16] This distinction will be utilised here to treat the doctrine of *Realpolitik* first in the traditionalist hands of Kissinger as statesman, and secondly in the work of modernist American commentators. These will then be joined by a third category of ultra-modernists or futurists.

Kissinger sought a stable, durable, structure of peace. There were three pillars to this structure: partnership with friendly nations, strength against potential aggressors and willingness to negotiate with former adversaries. Partnership in the shape of the Nixon Doctrine meant the allies doing more for themselves, and the United States reducing its commitments to a size determined by her interests rather than allowing commitments to dictate interests. Strength meant not primacy, but sufficiency, recognising that predominance undermined a relationship of security with other great powers rather than building it. 'Equal security' was the slogan of SALT. And willingness to negotiate stemmed from a theory that the way to deal with the communist world was to enmesh it in a network of relations with the Western world establishing a pattern of common interests that it would be difficult to disrupt. For the purposes of this exercise the Soviet Union and China were to be treated as states with interests rather than movements with ideologies, and the United States was to work on these interests by an astute application of the mechanisms of 'linkage': the connection of one policy with another until the adversary partner was caught in the Western web.

There were difficulties with this structure: the tenuous nature for a great power of a distinction between commitments and interests; the doubts about what 'strength' was and who had it; and the persistent failure of the mechanism of linkage; but it was a structure immediately recognisable from the viewpoint of *Realpolitik* established above. There is the same preoccupation with the state and with arrangements among the great powers as in the doctrine of *convenance*. There is the same priority assigned to security, and if the maintenance of the power of the state is not a task of 'incomparable grandeur', as Treitschke had it, it is still a high moral duty which sets aside the protests of ordinary morality. And there is the same notion of *raison d'état* as the ascendancy of limited aims over universalism. In the game of comparison with the figures of Kissinger's past, my selection for the early years of the Nixon administration is Castlereagh: in the distinction between internal and external affairs and the insistence on non-intervention – at least as a rule of great power relations (Castlereagh's conservatism not Metternich's); in the depiction of a world of interests rather than ideologies; and in the emphasis on reducing commitments – as if the United States were to behave towards the world as Britain once had towards Europe, as the state holding the balance but only intermittently becoming a weight in the scales. But when the Soviet Union seemed to show in Angola and elsewhere that it would not play by these rules, Kissinger moved back from interests to commitments, and from the Soviet Union as nation-state to the Soviet Union as ideologue. The stress, as recorded in Kissinger's memoirs, was now on the activity of the Soviet Union as mocking traditional rules like that of non-interference, and on the duty of the United States to define the limits of Soviet aspirations.[17]

Kissinger, in either of these versions, was unmistakably traditionalist. In the later Nixon–Ford years he was dragged into modernism willy-nilly, and learned the language of interdependence. The model of world politics as 'complex interdependence' has been fruitfully compared to the realist model that we have been discussing up to now in three ways.[18] In the first place, the realist assumption of the primacy and impenetrability of the state is replaced in complex interdependence by a description of the multiple channels connecting societies. Secondly, the realist preoccupation with the use or threat of force in international politics is compared to the reckoning by complex interdependence with the expanding international milieu for the interpretation of which the study of force is no guide. And in the third place, the realist image of a hierarchy of international issues, with security 'high' and welfare 'low', is contrasted with the treatment by the complex interdependence model of a multiplicity of issues not ordered in a pre-ordained hierarchy, but shifting according to the pattern of interdependence.

The significance of the modernists' model for the analysis of international politics is likewise threefold. If there is no issue – hierarchy with security matters coming automatically at the top, then the question of the agenda of international politics is not settled, and the matter of how it is settled becomes part of our subject-matter. Secondly, if power as military power has no particular impact on much that is at issue in the contemporary world, we can no longer investigate the subject in terms of the traditionalists' account of great power management of international politics. In particular, Kissinger's linkage breaks if power cannot be translated from one context to another. And in the third place, if states are not unified actors in international politics, distinguishing sharply between their internal and external affairs, then, to employ an honoured metaphor in the literature, the billiard balls are pocketed and we must start again.

Stanley Hoffmann sums up for the modernists with a kitchen rather than a games-room simile. 'In the traditional usage of power, states were like boiled eggs. War, the minute of truth, would reveal whether they (or which ones) were hard or soft. Interdependence breaks eggs into a vast omelet. It does not mean the end of conflict: I may want *my* egg to contribute a larger part of the omelet's size than *your* egg . . . But we all end in the same omelet.' Returning to the games-room, he adds a motto: 'You can harm me, and I you, but neither of us can retaliate fully without harming himself.'[19] The game is called the manipulation of interdependence.

How far have the modernists come from the theory of *Realpolitik*? The state is still the centre of political decision, but the decisions are made in a context which has changed their nature. The 'antimonies of diplomatico-strategic conduct' are now an increasingly elusive guide to the behaviour of states, and the milieu with which the state must now engage is one that undermines its autonomy through transnational penetration, and reduces its coherence through the multiplication of transgovernmental channels. On this account, *raison d'état* might be said to deserve its status as 'a fossil, a conscious archaism'.[20]

But no such transcendence has taken place in that part of the theory of *Realpolitik* which is concerned with the relationship between politics and morality. The transnational society which might be said to exist beyond the society of states in virtue of the phenomenon of complex interdependence has not, for the modernists looked at here, pulled them in the direction of cosmopolitan conceptions of right. Their language uses instead the traditional vocabulary of legitimacy. 'For international regimes to appear legitimate to [states at the bottom of hierarchies] they must perceive that they are receiving a significant share of joint gains.'[21]

International arrangements to cope with interdependence are to be shored up by common interests, rather than by common needs, or by a universal conception of justice. *Raison d'état* is not entirely fossilised.

Where the modernists have in some degree failed, we might expect the ultra-modernists to have succeeded in getting *raison d'état* into the museum where it belongs. But it is an important part of their argument that the radical reordering of the world that is necessary for human survival is something demanded as much by the common interests of states, as well as by individuals, as by the dictates of a universal morality. Thus, even before his conversion to global salvationism, Richard Falk wrote of the need for 'a new cynicism which turns out to look curiously like idealism', adding that 'a contemporary Machiavelli, perceiving the novel necessity for a community of mankind, might be dismissed by the best minds as recklessly utopian'.[22] This route to a world community will be tried out in the conclusion.

III

The argument of section II of this chapter was that the theory of *Realpolitik* endures in the doctrines of contemporary traditionalists, and, in a mildly rearranged form, in the outlook of the modernists, and even, through the doctrine of necessity, in the work of the ultra-modernists. The question for this conclusion is whether it is possible to get from interests to community, not the community of an international *eisteddfod* with people dressing up in national costume and linking arms with other cultures, nor that transnational association of 'complex interdependence' which catches people in the net of world society, but a real community to which people owe their allegiance.

For the purposes of the discussion that follows society will be taken to mean a pattern among individuals, or notional individuals like states, that exists in virtue of their common interests, and a community to mean a pattern that exists in virtue of their common will. The idea that a pattern existing in virtue of common interests might endure sufficiently to warrant the label society is not an obvious or uncontested one, but in relation to international society it has its starting-place in Hobbes's pronouncement that the international anarchy is, because it upholds the industry of the subjects of sovereigns, more bearable than anarchy among individual human beings. This is partly because of the strength of states. They are not vulnerable to a single deadly blow as individuals are. It is partly too because of the inequality of states, admitting the possibility that their affairs can be ordered according to the principle that might is right.[23] And it is partly because of the impetus to self-restraint given by recognition of a freemasonry of states: 'each state has an essentially domestic interest in self-restraint, since, should it implicate its population in all-out wars of extermination, the subjects' duty of obedience to it would disappear'.[24] Interests held in common then become reciprocal: the principle of state sovereignty might be rendered 'you order your population and I will order mine: you stay out of my affairs and I will stay out of yours'. Further down the same path is the institution of the balance of power to preserve the independence of states, and the articulation of an international interest in its preservation. And so on.

Against this complacent vision of the construction of an international society stands Rousseau's doubt that *raison d'état* could so easily become reason of states, that some magical conception of the common interest could lay down a similar pattern of restraint to all the actors in international politics. But it is the complacent vision that seems to me to inform the schemes of the modernists: in the search for stable regimes to manage the networks of interdependence; in the requirements of leadership that regimes not be sacrificed for short-term gains; and in the mechanism of bargaining among actors for the establishment of legitimate arrangements.[25] The prominence of *Realpolitik* in the doctrine of the modernists is nowhere better expressed than in the idea that Third World demands on the North–South chessboard serve Northern interests by giving them a means of leverage over the South, and an opportunity for them to co-ordinate their strategy towards the South.[26] Southern demands if met would serve the Northern interest in integrating the South more thoroughly into the system, and if the South had not made the demands the North might reasonably have pressed them to do so.

In all this, there is still no sense of community in the form that it has been defined above. 'The model of community', says Stanley Hoffmann, 'is as irrelevant as it has been for more than four centuries. There is no equivalent of the universal church.'[27] But it is interesting to note that the adherents to this irrelevant model can enlist Hobbes on its behalf. It is a commonplace observation of contemporary international politics that the advent of nuclear weapons has reduced states to the position of men in the state of nature, the prospect of their total destruction equalising their misery in just the condition of Hobbes's individual.[28] And the possibility of nuclear disaster has more recently been joined by the various dimensions of the ecological crisis as pressures for the establishment of a global community. A famous account of the politics of the ecological crisis, focused on the problem of population but applicable more generally, has been given in Garrett Hardin's analysis of the 'tragedy of the commons'.[29] There is no conflict between the interests of individual herdsmen and those of the group of herdsmen using the commons so long as it has the capacity to accommodate additional animals without affecting the grazing of the animals already pastured. But once this point is passed, the tragedy of the commons is set in train, for while it is in the interests of an individual herdsman to add to his stock of animals, his yield increasing albeit at a reduced rate, the interests of the group of herdsmen is damaged by diminishing marginal yields. So long as an individual's gain outweighs his costs he continues to add stock to the commons. But the inevitable result of the overgrazing that follows is damage done to the interests of every herdsman. The failure to articulate a group interest, and to create an institution to enforce it has reduced the welfare of each individual. This is Hobbes. If each individual pursues his own interest in the absence of government, then the resulting war of all against all is more miserable than the peace and security produced by government.[30] Enter the Leviathan to protect our interests by overawing us.

But if states are likely, for a variety of reasons, to neglect their true interest in surrendering their sovereignty to a common power, we are back to the problem of building a community bit by bit rather than producing one out of a contractual hat. This is the province of the functionalists, placing their faith in what Martin Wight calls the modern substitute for the law of nature – the law of common material interest.[31] Wight does not doubt the reality of a common interest in planned global economic development to meet the universal demand for social justice, but declares that this 'does not touch the problem of power' which dictates that any state will see global welfare as of lesser importance than, and derivative from, the maintenance of its own power. For this reason he concludes that a common moral obligation is probably a more fruitful social doctrine than the idea of a common material interest, and finds in the fraction that it may deflect powers from the confrontation of power politics 'the difference between the jungle and the traditions of Europe'.

What this pessimistic doctrine plays down is the extent to which common obligations might emerge from the business of looking after common interests. Kenneth Boulding is less pessimistic. He finds in what he calls the 'grants economy' something which cannot be explained without reference to some notion of a community of interest. 'If A gives B something without expecting anything in return, the inference must be drawn that B is "part" of A or that A and B together are parts of a larger system of interests and organizations.'[32] Whether the grant is given out of pity or patronage, it is a mark of the spread of a sense of community from the national to the world arena. This process is as yet sketchy and uneven, but that is no warrant to dismiss the idea of community out of hand. The traditionalist preoccupation with a legitimate interstate order, and the modernist search for a way of legitimising transnational regimes, might both be counted as evidence for a recognition of a 'larger system of interests and organizations'. Reason of state, reason of system, reason of regimes, all this is far short of the world community which the ultra-modernists urge us, in the utopian tradition, at once to recognise and to create. Nor is it based on a theory of common obligation, and it has no binding power stronger than the separate interpretation of particular interests. Moreover, it is an arrangement of affairs that might lead as much to conflict as to harmony. But without common interests, or at least the perception of such by the makers of decisions, it is hard to imagine the creation of any world community at all. Common moral obligation may, it is true, be a more fruitful social doctrine than that of common material interests, but it can only bear fruit when embedded in the soil of interest. It seems perverse to disconnect the two. Either *Realpolitik* and world community, or no world community.

NOTES: CHAPTER 5

1 A. J. P. Taylor, *Bismarck: The Man and the Statesman*, (London: Hamish Hamilton, 1955), p. 265.
2 See Chapter 10 below.
3 See W. F. Church, *Richelieu and Reason of State* (Princeton, NJ: Princeton University Press, 1972), and Sir Herbert Butterfield, *Raison d'État: The Relations between Morality and Government* (The First Martin Wight Memorial Lecture, University of Sussex, 23 April 1975).
4 W. F. Church, op. cit., p. 200.
5 H. A. Kissinger, 'The White Revolutionary: reflections on Bismarck', *Daedalus*, vol. 97, no. 3 (Summer 1968), p. 908.
6 F. Meinecke, *Machiavellism* (London: Routledge & Kegan Paul, 1962), p. 88.
7 H. von Treitschke, *Politics* (New York: Harcourt Brace Jovanovitch, 1963), p. 54.
8 W. F. Church, op. cit., pp. 44, 91, 131.
9 A. J. P. Taylor, op. cit., p. 21.
10 F. Meinecke, op. cit., p. 1.
11 H. Butterfield, op. cit., p. 10.
12 See R. W. Sterling, *Ethics in a World of Power* (Princeton, NJ: Princeton University Press, 1958).
13 R. M. Hare, *Applications of Moral Philosophy* (London: Macmillan, 1972), p. 22.
14 F. Meinecke, op. cit., p. 9.
15 F. Meinecke, op. cit., ch. 11.
16 See for example R. O. Keohane and J. Nye, *Power and Interdependence* (Boston, Mass.: Little, Brown, 1977), and S. Hoffmann, *The State of War* (New York: Praeger, 1965).
17 H. A. Kissinger, *The White House Years* (London: Weidenfeld & Nicolson and Michael Joseph, 1979), pp. 117, 119.
18 R. O. Keohane and J. Nye, op. cit., ch. 2.
19 S. Hoffmann, op. cit., pp. 117, 124.
20 H. Butterfiield, op. cit., p. 7.
21 R. O. Keohane and J. Nye, op. cit., p. 235.
22 R. A. Falk, *Legal Order in a Violent World* (Princeton, NJ: Princeton University Press, 1968), pp. 111–15.
23 H. Bull, 'Society and anarchy in international relations', in H. Butterfield and M. Wight (eds), *Diplomatic Investigations* (London: Allen & Unwin, 1966), pp. 35–52.
24 S. Hoffmann, op. cit., p. 61.

25   R. O. Keohane and J. Nye, op. cit., ch. 8.
26   See Tony Smith, 'Changing configurations of power in north south relations since 1945', *International Organisation*, vol. 31, no. 1 (Winter 1977).
27   S. Hoffmann, *Primacy or World Order* (New York: McGraw Hill, 1978), p. 144.
28   See for example David P. Gauthier, *The Logic of Leviathan* (Oxford: Clarendon Press, 1969).
29   G. Hardin, 'The tragedy of the commons', *Science*, vol. 162, no. 3859 (13 December 1968), pp. 1243-8.
30   N. Taylor, *Anarchy and Cooperation* (London: Wiley, 1976).
31   M. Wight, *Power Politics* (London: Penguin, 1978).
32   K. Boulding, 'The concept of world interest', in R. Falk and S. Menlovitz (eds), *The Strategy of World Order*, Vol. IV (New York: World Law Fund, 1966), pp. 494–516.

6

A Community of Terror?

BARRIE PASKINS

Since time immemorial the hatred of man for man has been sufficient to motivate us to persist in battle to the point of complete mutual annihilation. But war has often ended short of this, with one party seeking to surrender rather than be destroyed and another being prepared to grant 'peace' terms whose punishment of the defeated stops short of genocide. Even when, as in the Old Testament or in Rome's dealings with Carthage, whole polities have been put to the sword, the human disaster has been limited by the existence of other communities untouched by the massacre.

What is new since 1945 is not the depth of hatred that pervades international relations but technological innovations which have made every civilised community simultaneously vulnerable to annihilating bombardment, and the incorporation of these innovations into great power strategy in such a way that we now look to the risk of high-speed destruction for the security of our nations and persons. What does this development mean for international relations? Does the destruction of societies by nuclear war constitute a *summum malum* so probable and fearsome as to force the most 'realistic' of statesmen to participate in the creation of a genuine international community as an alternative to disaster?

The answer depends partly on what we mean by community. If what is meant is a common feeling of terror and alarm in face of the bomb, then a modicum of terrified community does seem to exist. But surely community means something more than common feeling? Membership of a community alters the expectations one is entitled to have of one's fellow members. For example, if a golf club is worth calling a community, then a playing member is entitled to expect of his fellow playing members some interest in golf and some readiness to join in a game. Such expectations would not be reasonable with respect to random members of the general public. If the expectations of the golfer are disappointed by his fellow playing members, he is entitled to complain, 'If they weren't interested in golf and a game, they shouldn't have joined'.

Similarly, I suggest, if there is an international community to which fear of nuclear weapons has given rise, then it ought to be possible to point to the difference in international relations that this community makes in terms of the mutual expectations that are legitimate in virtue of it, and would not be legitimate otherwise. What I am asking, therefore, is not whether nuclear weapons have affected the behaviour of states – of course they have – but whether there is an ethos of mutual understanding to which nuclear weapons have given rise. Legitimate complaints of bad behaviour are the issue, rather than good conduct which is the product of mere self-interest as distinct from a community created by fear of the *summum malum*. To investigate this question, let us first recall some well-known facts and ideas about nuclear weapons.

I

In 1938 the theoretical possibility of nuclear weapons was unknown to governments. Refugees from Hitler's Europe, pondering the appalling possibility that the Third Reich might be the first to acquire nuclear weapons, persuaded the British and, with difficulty, the American authorities to devote a modest budget to guard against this possibility. Advances were made despite the scepticism of eminent Americans, and without further strategic or moral deliberation the Manhattan Project was begun. Until late 1944 its rationale was the possibility of Hitler being first to the bomb. There was plenty to do without thinking beyond the race against Germany. Then it was found that the danger was unreal. Hitler's conservative preference for ballistics, aided perhaps by triumph of conscience or failure of imagination in his remaining physicists and in Albert Speer, had resulted in its being quite impossible that a German bomb would be ready for the war. The Manhattan Project continued, perhaps from bureaucratic inertia. It survived the German surrender. Some of the bomb's creators were invited to suggest uses for it. They did so in ignorance of Japanese peace-feelers put out as early as 1944 and known to some members of the US administration. They suggested a demonstration test to intimidate the Japanese but this failed to convince the authorities – the Japanese might not come; the demonstration bomb might fail to explode; the demonstration might be insufficiently impressive to cow the enemy. A less unorthodox approach was available. The strategy of bombing cities from the air had been in the making in Europe and America since 1916 and vast quantities of high explosive had been dropped on Germany and Japan. In August 1945 the US Air Force could fly anywhere over Japan without facing significant resistance. To drop the bomb in anger was easy and intellectually straightforward. The bombing of Hiroshima and (ahead of schedule) Nagasaki, together with Soviet entry into the war against Japan, at last elicited surrender from an already defeated but stubbornly resistant foe.[1]

Thus the bomb stole upon us unawares. It was already among us, had already killed tens of thousands and played a part, however obscure, in ending a brutal world war before anything that could be called an international community had any opportunity to reflect upon it. Its invention had not required sustained thought about international relations because it was in response to a fearsome pariah from whom the United Nations required nothing short of unconditional surrender. Its use required no drastic new decisions of the military or political authorities because it fitted so neatly into a battleplan already in operation. After Nagasaki the bomb was a brute fact which the international community might face or evade but had not created and could not think away without concrete political action. Faced nowadays with elaborate and sophisticated ideas about how the bomb can be incorporated into world order, one is tempted to think of it as an instrument of politics. It assuredly did not begin so, however things may now stand, and one must entertain the hypothesis that the international community may have failed to find a place in the world for the brute fact on which it stumbled unawares.

In the three-and-a-half decades since Nagasaki the development in quantity and quality of nuclear weapons has been breathtaking, while four, five, or six states have breached the US monopoly and another thirty are thought to be capable of doing so in a relatively short time given the political will. In 1945 the USA had, after successful testing, only two atom bombs. No more would have been available for several months if the Japanese had not surrendered when they did, and one reason which has been suggested to explain why Nagasaki was bombed ahead of schedule alleges fears that in case of delay Japan would have guessed there were only two bombs and continued fighting. Today even the smallest declared nuclear weapons programme has weapons many times more powerful and several times more numerous than the USA possessed in 1945. The American and Soviet arsenals each contain tens of thousands of warheads with yields up to 2,500 times those of the bombs that devastated Japan. The series of revolutions in delivery system have been equally important. In 1945 the Americans had no option but to make a weapon for dropping by heavy bomber. Today bombers, land-based and submarine-based systems permit each of the superpowers, especially the USA, to feel that massive redundancy increases its security. To rival an established nuclear-weapons state, a newcomer must somehow match extremely sophisticated delivery systems. In the case of the superpowers, such a third-party challenge is if anything even more inconceivable than matching their stockpile of warheads. But it should be remembered that the development of delivery systems which has produced some types wholly beyond the reach of any but the greatest military powers has also produced readily exportable systems capable of delivering the rather crude and relatively large warheads which are easiest to make; some of these are ambiguous in the sense of having other uses for which they might be exported, and are therefore singularly difficult for opponents of nuclear proliferation to contain.

The development of warheads and delivery systems has been associated with a variety of strategic ideas, the best known of which in the West are American. Let us review briefly four of these: containment, flexibility, sufficiency and vigilance. *Containment*[2] represents us to ourselves as facing an expansionist opponent who must be expected to be trying to augment his malign influence throughout the world. The opponent may be identified as the USSR, or as something less easily delineated such as 'communism' or 'Russian communism'. Because intentions can change overnight and the closed society poses even greater intelligence problems than are inevitable in politics, much weight is unavoidably given by adherents of containment theory to worst-case analysis of the opponent's capacity to prosecute that expansionism which we are required to oppose. The general idea of containment does not in strict logic entail military containment, but it makes arguments for global military measures hard to resist by the omnipresence it attributes to powers against whom some area of military opposition is all but inevitable. There is an uncannily neat fit between containment's intimation of the need for global military measures and the global impact that would undoubtedly result from nuclear war.

The emphasis on *flexibility*[3] is often linked to President John Kennedy's demand for other options in addition to holocaust and surrender, but even at the height of Dulles's strategy of massive retaliation the American authorities always wanted to insist on the greatest feasible freedom of manoeuvre for the President. Perhaps the peculiar genius of Kennedy and MacNamara lay in connecting this perennial desire of all politicians to technological innovation and bureaucratic reform. The idea behind flexible response and kindred strategies is that one must seek to have available such technologies as are needed to maximise the range of strategic options. A variety of reasons for such maximising can be given: freedom of manoeuvre for the President; avoidance of a credibility gap which may result in the enemy supposing they can practise (for example) salami tactics against an alliance paralysed between suicide and surrender; reassurance of allies jittery about US commitment and potentially dangerous if sufficiently alarmed. Whatever reasons support it, the desire for flexibility motivates high military expenditures because more systems cost more money.

Sufficiency is attainable, according to MacNamara and others, in that there comes a point where the USA can inflict so much damage on the enemy whatever that enemy does that a further increase in weapons is pointless. If this idea is accepted, there is a basis for curbing parts of the defence budget on the ground that one enjoys sufficiency in certain types of system. Such an argument could be deployed in one direction by a budget-cutter, in quite another by contending that funds freed by sufficiency in one area should be reallocated elsewhere in the defence field in the interests of flexibility. Confidence of sufficiency at all of the levels required for flexibility will be very hard to sustain so long as the globalism of containment prevails and finds direct translation into the military sphere.

By '*vigilance*', I mean to recall the famous article in *Foreign Affairs* 1959[4] in which Albert Wohlstetter argued that the balance of terror which is thought to exist between the USA and USSR is *delicate*, that is, susceptible of upset by technological innovation. Concern for vigilance derives from the premises of flexibility. In principle, one could either affirm or deny that nuclear deterrence is semi-automatic. One could affirm this on the ground that the dangers are so great, obvious and inescapable that no one is going to run the sort of risks that might lead to nuclear war. Such a position would tend to favour relatively low nuclear defence budgets because flexibility would be pointless, and could perhaps be implemented in a way that would avoid the tendency of sophisticated deterrent systems to increase the probability of accidental nuclear war.[5] One could deny that nuclear deterrence is semi-automatic in various ways, perhaps most importantly by asserting that there are grey areas of uncertainty where the powers will test one another and advantage will go against the weaker. Such a position would give a foothold to demands for flexibility. Wohlstetter builds on denial of the view that deterrence is semi-automatic. If the horrific potential of pretty well any nuclear weapons system is insufficient, any system can be rendered inadequate by technological change. What I am calling 'vigilance' is the demand that one be ever-ready to respond to technological innovation by counter-innovation that will preserve flexibility. Vigilance need not always be a high-spending notion, but it always threatens to subvert sufficiency by reference to the time dimension in which weapons can be counted on to become insufficient relative to new technology.

Containment, flexibility, sufficiency and vigilance are American ideas. What corresponds in Soviet thinking to the idea of containment appears to be a sense of encirclement, of a coalition of enemies pressing on the very borders of the homeland and threatening subversion within. Ideology makes it difficult to refuse requests for aid from self-proclaimed Marxists and resentment of American pre-eminence draws the USSR into wider global ambitions. The tendency of containment to make every point on the earth's surface (and seabed) into a vital Western interest does not seem to have an equivalent in the thinking of a state which has experienced onslaughts within its own borders this century of a kind that the USA has never faced.

The Soviets seem to have their own ideas about flexibility: they seem to plan for it, but to have radically different ideas about the options they want and how these are interrelated. Where the West speaks of an escalation ladder beginning with non-nuclear combat options proceeding via tactical nuclear weapons to increasingly massive strategic nuclear bombardments, the Soviet plan appears to involve early use of massive nuclear firepower with no sharp distinction between tactical and strategic nuclear systems and a substantial use of chemical weapons. The USSR is said not to accept the idea of sufficiency but to favour a war-winning strategy involving the high-budget assumption that more systems might come in useful (if only for the purpose of redundancy, as a hedge against massive failure of weapons). Vigilance does seem to be favoured by the USSR.

The other nuclear weapons states are incapable of containment (except as junior alliance partners), cannot afford flexibility, find enormous difficulty affording vigilance (c.f. the anguished UK Trident decision) and face economic disciplines that render the notion of sufficiency otiose. Non-nuclear-weapons states appear uninterested in the strategic ideas we have been reviewing. Their commentary concentrates on 'vertical proliferation' conceived in terms of crude numbers. Perhaps they consider the strategic niceties unworthy of being taken at face value.

In this section we have surveyed the unpromising origins and current distribution of nuclear weapons, together with some strategic ideas about them which have played some part at some level of debate in their evolution. In the next section I relate this material to the notions of common fear and community with which this chapter began.

II

A certain view of nuclear weapons is very widely shared and may even appear incontrovertible. According to it, nuclear weapons have been used but only in conditions so different from those now prevailing that we can derive no lessons beyond a sober recognition of the extreme unpleasantness of these weapons and the readiness of a power enjoying monopoly in them to use them in a war already massively brutal in other ways. Nuclear weapons now are dangerous in virtue of their numbers and readiness for use, but the danger is shrouded in uncertainty. It seems that no one wants them to be used, and that considerable precautions have been taken against accidents. So it would not be an accurate reflection of our feelings to say that we are sitting on a time-bomb. We feel that the danger need not materialise if everyone is sensible, and we blow hot and cold about the reliability of the requisite good sense. We also attach a certain symbolism to these weapons. All and only the confessed nuclear weapons states are Permanent Members of the UN Security Council. There is no agreed link between the weapons and the seats but the coincidence is very often mentioned, especially by critics, as a suitable indication of the status the weapons confer or represent. We are all uncertain of the extent to which these weapons confer, the extent to which they merely represent greatness. To the danger and glamour we attribute to nuclear weapons must be added a feeling that these are not dirty weapons. Especially since the Partial Test Ban Treaty drove warhead testing underground, the common feeling about nuclear weapons has been quite different from the common revulsion against biological and (at least in a wide segment of Western opinion) chemical weapons. So long as deterrence does not 'fail', nuclear weapons are part of the core that fuels politics: it is not felt *shameful* to possess them. Yet for all our acceptance of the existence of nuclear weapons, we hanker after their abolition. Remarkably enough, each of those envied Permanent Members is on record as favouring eventual abolition. That it should be felt worthwhile to make declarations about nuclear weapons as distinct from the millennium of complete and general disarmament attests our fixation on this technology.

The great fear is, of course, that as a result of accident, miscalculation, or proliferation deterrence will fail. The word 'proliferation' is evidence of such fears that are common to us all. It brings together the spread of nuclear weapons to more states ('horizontal proliferation') and the increasing quantity and/or quality of the existing nuclear armouries ('vertical proliferation'). This grouping together of far-from-obviously-connected phenomena finds official expression in the Non-Proliferation Treaty. The underlying idea seems to be roughly as follows. In security policy, states have equal rights. Ergo if some states have a right to nuclear weapons, all have. This right is established for the few by brute facts of history. But it is a problem for us all because we are dismayed at the prospect of the uncontrolled legitimate spread of these weapons. So what are we to say? Well, what we need is a treaty, that typical representation of the (fictional) equality of states, and the treaty must link the weaponry which has to be accepted and that whose spread we do not want to legitimise lightly. On reflection, the treaty must therefore take the form of an agreement between the haves to move towards abolition and the have-nots to remain in a state which they have the right to leave.

To support and elucidate this speculative reading of the treaty, let us look at a French argument which purports to legitimise the spread of nuclear weapons. Horizontal proliferation is not to be feared, so the argument runs, because the bomb confers responsibility and thereby establishes stability wherever it spreads. If nuclear weapons have helped to keep peace between the USA and the USSR, this is not because these powers have displayed any special wisdom but because the technology imposes restraint on any power with the slightest prudence. A decently balanced spread of the bomb will create further areas of peace.

One can of course argue against this view. Perhaps nuclear weapons are less important for peace than it suggests. Perhaps transfer of command and control systems is less straightforward than it assumes. It fails to explain how peace will be preserved if a state to which the bomb has spread collapses into civil war. Perhaps one does not want to see international relations frozen to the degree the argument assumes – perhaps one wants to leave room for non-nuclear war to remain a yeast of history. Perhaps the argument underestimates the factors other than peace-preservation that attach the present nuclear-weapons states to their nuclear arsenals, factors such as membership of a small clique that might deform any peace-preserving spread and/or block inference from the *status quo* to premises concerning peace-preservation. And one can readily imagine patterns of horizontal proliferation which would be extremely hazardous, one state acquiring a lead sufficient to pre-empt a long-term enemy by early nuclear bombardment; without an incredible degree of disinterested even-handedness, one might argue, such imbalances would be all but inevitable.

Yet the precise merits of the spread-for-peace idea are beside the point. What is interesting is that the idea is publicly available, not evidently foolish, yet quite without influence. Even France has not acted on it as foreign policy. Why should such an admirably clear idea be so lacking in resonance? At least four factors seem to be at work. First, there just is agreement among states that nuclear weaponry is undesirable and, other things being equal, not to be proliferated. Anyone with the fear of nuclear weapons we sketched earlier cannot take the spread-for-peace idea seriously without the strongest pressure: it is too lightweight, too much of a witty *jeu*. Second, deployment of nuclear weapons is a heavy strain on even the most flourishing economy. This puts a large obstacle in the way of any broad-brush theoretical argument. Third, there are interesting states which gain by the *status quo*. Both Israel and South Africa in their different ways gain leverage by US reluctance to have them breach the taboo against horizontal proliferation. A general legitimation of spread would subvert the assumptions that give force to their 'have we, haven't we' postures. Fourth, as things stand now the acquisition of nuclear weapons is an act of high drama. Its availability as a rhetorical figure should not be under-estimated. It is far from clear that states which may be prepared to bear the economic burden of going nuclear would stand to gain from loss of this rhetorical figure. In view of these four factors, the communitarian implications of the word 'proliferation' may be more far-reaching, may confer more stability on the *status quo*, than might at first sight appear.

III

Thus far, I have been considering the common fear of nuclear weapons in general and more especially relative to horizontal proliferation. Let us now turn to the strategic ideas outlined in section II, and ask what bearing there is upon them of the general notion of community sketched at the outset. Have definite mutual expectations emerged as a context for containment, flexibility, sufficiency and vigilance or do these strategic ideas operate in a way unconstrained by any 'community of states'?

The idea of containment, and the corresponding Soviet sense of encirclement, would seem to be inescapably opposed to the construction of definite mutual understandings among the powers concerned. The expectations constitutive of community eliminate the need for constant recalculation of antagonistic interests; negatively they remove many fearful possibilities from the options to be taken seriously, positively they create new possibilities whose availability is a welcome consequence of mutuality. Containment, by contrast, requires us to construe every political event, every spot of the earth's surface, as fraught with (shifting) danger. Still worse, in so far as containment identifies the opponent not as a particular state (for example, the USSR) but as something more shadowy and pervasive (for example, 'communism'), the prospects of community shrink and powers with whom one's relations are difficult are driven *by one's own concepts* into common cause against one. (At the time of writing, for example, containment of the shadow enemy is constitutive of the extremely bad relations between the USA and Vietnam.) Thus, so long as containment and strategic ideas akin to it dominate foreign and military policy, they rule out those mutual expectations which I have argued constitute the real substance of community.

Flexibility and vigilance make the position still worse. Concerned as they are with technology, they enjoin adherents to increase the complexity and flux of something which is intrinsically ambiguous. Any weapons system has a variety of uses. The greater the variety of systems, the greater are the possibilities of being in doubt as to the nature of the threat posed to one by any power with whom one's military relations are not perfectly harmonious. I am not speaking here of misperception, as though a possessor of weapons could know its own true intentions which might be misinterpreted by outsiders. Regardless of the extent to which states can be credited with the capacity to have definite intentions concerning their weaponry, the systems available to them are necessarily an object of speculation in their opponents. Flexibility and vigilance encourage this speculation to proceed in a direction wholly alien to the achievement of definite mutual expectations. This tendency interacts with containment, political events rendered still more ambiguous and alarming by technology, technology still more imponderable by political events construed in the containment mode.

What of sufficiency? Some definite achievements can be credited to this idea, notably the Anti-Ballistic Missile (ABM) Treaty by which the USA and USSR limited to very modest proportions anti-ballistic missile defences that unrestrained should by the time of writing have prompted even higher levels of defence spending and even more strategically alarming technological innovations than we have in fact experienced. For a while it appeared to some that the ABM Treaty provided a model for the construction of genuine mutual understandings in arms control. But it has proved possible for critics in the USA to bring under enormous pressure the idea of mutual assured destruction which is the strategic rationale for the ABM Treaty. Highly technical arguments have proved to enjoy great political sway, convincing a large and influential body of opinion that Soviet technological innovation threatens US second-strike capability in a way that requires massive new American expenditures. The systems to be procured by the US are of a kind to put pressure on the USSR to return to missile defences, or initiate huge new batteries of offensive weaponry. The point that matters for present purposes is that this political controversy has been conducted in terms that exhibit sufficiency as a (very vulnerable) technical idea rather than as a (relatively stable) communitarian understanding. Sufficiency seems to be emerging as powerless to restrain the capacity of containment, flexibility and vigilance to pulverise the construction of mutual expectations on which the USA and USSR can rely in their dealings with one another and with the rest of the world.

What are the implications of all this for the idea that the destruction of societies by nuclear war constitutes a *summum malum* so probable and fearsome as to force the most 'realistic' of statesmen to participate in the creation of a genuine international community as an alternative to disaster? If what is meant by community is no more than a common feeling of terror and alarm in face of the bomb then a modicum of terrified community does seem to exist and, as I have tried to suggest in my discussion of non-proliferation, may have some real impact on what happens in the world. But I began by expressing my view that anything worth calling a community must be more structured than the existence of mere common feeling requires. I claimed that a necessary condition of community is mutual expectations which are legitimate in virtue of that which is being called 'community' and would not be legitimate without it. I have argued that containment, flexibility and vigilance are inimical to community in this sense, and that sufficiency seems powerless to resist the anti-communitarian pressure of containment, flexibility and vigilance. Nuclear weapons are not going to vanish and, short of major war, there may, if we are lucky, still be time for the most 'realistic' of statesmen to be pushed by the *summum malum* to participate in the creation of a genuine international community. But it does not seem to be happening yet.

NOTES: CHAPTER 6

1 Barrie Paskins and Michael Dockrill, *The Ethics of War* (London: Duckworth, 1979). Chapter 1 provides a fuller account of the origin of the nuclear age.
2 Daniel Yergin, *Shattered Peace: The Origins of the Cold War and the National Security State* (Harmondsworth: Penguin, 1980), furnishes a painstaking even-handed account of the origin of containment thinking.
3 R. F. Weigley, *The American Way of War* (London: Collier Macmillan, 1973), pp. 363–477, provides a useful guide to the background of flexibility, sufficiency and what I am calling 'vigilance'.
4 'The delicate balance of terror', *Foreign Affairs*, vol. XXXVIII (January 1959), pp. 211–34.
5 My essay in Geoffrey Goodwin (ed.), *Principle and Prudence: Ethics and Nuclear Deterrence* (London: Croom Helm, 1982), seeks to elaborate the idea of semi-automatic nuclear deterrence, and to derive a unilateralist policy implication from it.

7
The Liberal Economy

JAMES MAYALL

These days, the economy hovers like an unwelcome incubus over all our imaginings. Whether we are poor trying to get rich, or rich trying to stay rich, there is no escape. It has not always been so. In other ages economic issues did not dominate public debate about the ends of human life and the programme to be followed for achieving these ends as they now do. Earlier chapters in this book have explored the setting in which economic ideas assumed their current dominance in social and political thought.[1] In this chapter I discuss the implications of economic thought for ideas about community in international relations.

There is, however, an initial difficulty. The main thrust of modern economics has been to separate the discipline from philosophy using a combination of empiricism and formal logic for this purpose. But to ask what is the nature or purpose of a human community is to ask a stubbornly philosophical question, that is, one which cannot be unambiguously answered by reference to empirical or formal knowledge.[2] Of course most distinguished economists have always acknowledged the ultimate dependence of their discipline on shared, that is, community values. As Professor Joan Robinson has put it, 'any economic system requires a set of rules, an ideology to justify them, and a conscience in the individual which makes him strive to carry them out'.[3] It is from this foundation, she suggests, that hypotheses are drawn which, unlike metaphysical or ideological propositions, are capable of empirical investigation. Nevertheless it has been the constant effort of modern economists to slip their metaphysical rein and to establish economics as an unambiguous positive science.

In practice the positivist claims of economics might not matter if economies were always coextensive with nation-states, if economic and political systems exactly mirrored one another. That is not, however, the case. It is true that the development of economics as a putative science has coincided with the consolidation of state power and the ubiquitous encroachment of state authorities into areas of social regulation which, in the West at least, were previously regarded as falling within the private rather than the public domain. Simultaneously, however, the integration of world markets has seriously weakened the ability of governments to achieve the economic goals which they set themselves within their own jurisdiction. In other words since the economic system now embraces states in general there is a need for both rules and a justifying ideology to sustain them. Moreover, this ideology – to follow Joan Robinson's logic – cannot be provided from within economics itself.

Where then can it be found? In the final section of this chapter I shall argue that the major economic problems in international relations in one way or another all raise the question of justice, a question which has been unpopular in economics since the middle ages. To talk about justice, of what is owed by men to each other, is necessarily to examine the nature, purpose and possibility of human community. The question cannot be answered, therefore, unambiguously or merely on the basis of technical criteria. In modern economic thought, however, two powerful answers have been advanced which challenge this view. The first proposed that a natural community of interests would be brought about by the operation of free markets; the second that since nature was unreliable, the same end could be achieved by deliberate and enlightened management by government authorities. It is to these arguments that I turn first.

I

The concept of community is not of central concern to either of the two rival traditions of economic thought which have dominated the modern world, the one fathered by Adam Smith, the other by Karl Marx. In both, however, communitarian assumptions are built into the foundations of the theory. By looking forward to a time when human relations would be governed under the formula 'from each according to his capacity to each according to his need', Marx employed a powerful communitarian vision to fix the terminal point of his historical and philosophical system. But in Marxist philosophy this vision serves to establish a negative criterion, that is, one which determines the absence of true community in existing social, political and economic arrangements. For Marx all such arrangements are based on conflict. On the other side Adam Smith was primarily concerned to show how existing arrange-ments could be made to conform with the requirements of 'natural liberty'. In so doing he presented free commerce as an essentially collaborative enterprise.[4]

No doubt the principal reason why neither the classical economists nor the Marxists faced the question of community directly is that at the time it did not seem necessary. The important task was to liberate economic thought from the stifling constraints of intellectual orthodoxy. And in the theories against which Smith rebelled, and which in consequence Marx was able to ignore, the primacy of politics over economics, the state over society and reason of state over private interest was assumed and justified.

In the process of liberation from this orthodoxy there were two revolutionary developments: the severing of the economy from both the polity and society at large, and what was necessary first, the 'discovery' of the division of labour. Smith maintained that the division of labour was causally derived from the human propensity to exchange and that, further, at a certain stage in its development individuals became greatly dependent on society for subsistence. It was from this latter argument that the idea of the supremacy of the market emerged, an idea which was in turn eventually to yield the important analytical fiction of perfect competition. As he put it, at this stage every man becomes 'in some measure a merchant and the society itself grows to be what is properly a commercial society'.[5] It is at this stage also that, for analytical purposes, a wedge is driven between the economy and political society.

Marx, and many later critics of classical liberalism, have held that this separation of economics from politics was merely a deceit, a form of moral blindness. It is important to recall, therefore, that the reconciliation of private interest with the public good through the mechanism of the market was originally seen as a solution to an intractable moral problem. As Peter Cain has reminded us, classical economics developed within a particular moral context.[6] In the philosophy of Adam Smith and his followers it was axiomatic that freedom from restraint would allow a society to evolve 'which would be regulated by a moral code implanted in men divinely and this would find expression in a system of natural justice . . . These natural laws were to provide the framework within which individuals could cooperate with each other on equal terms and on the principle of the division of labour.' The great advantage of this scheme was that it reconciled the individual to the nation and the nation to mankind. Ricardo celebrates rather than explains this famous reconciliation in the following way:

'Under a system of perfectly free commerce, each country naturally devotes its capital and labour to such employment as are most beneficial to each. This pursuit of individual advantage is admirably connected with the universal good of the whole. By stimulating industry, by rewarding ingenuity, and by using most efficaciously the peculiar powers bestowed by nature, it distributes labour most effectively and most economically; while by increasing the general mass of productions, it diffuses general benefits, and binds together by one common tie of interest and intercourse, the universal society of nations throughout the civilized world.'[7]

It is easy to see now that the reconciliation represents a powerful myth rather than a scientific law: it cannot dissolve the problem of obligation because it is obviously impossible to be responsible for a mechanism which is embedded in nature. On the other hand, given the difficulty of securing agreement between separate political communities the resort to mechanism had obvious practical advantages. Economic liberalism affirmed the need for a political structure of a definite kind with specific but limited functions. In positing laws of the market, of supply and demand and comparative advantage, it was rooted in a powerful individualism. The laws were all dependent on the notion of a man as a self-centred, rational economic optimiser. But precisely because man was that, all men were: a world of market laws implied, at least potentially, a world market and therefore potentially a community of mankind.

Meanwhile, however, men continued to live in separate states which frequently, if inconveniently, refused to acknowledge that they were bound by 'one common tie of interest' and which, since they could hardly be wished out of existence, had to be ascribed a legitimate place in the liberal scheme. Essentially this was achieved by confining the state to barracks. In other words governments were to confine themselves to maintaining and policing the framework within which the natural law could operate. And since the threat came from irrational obstruction, the framework was defined as a system of negatives, non-interference in the market, non-discriminatory trade, and so on. For the system to operate to maximum efficiency, however, that is, along the lines suggested by Ricardo, there was one vital prerequisite – peace between nations.

What if the peace was not kept? The short answer is that the liberal system, with its potential for the construction of a world commercial community, would lapse at that point. And in so far as defence was to be preferred to opulence, as Smith held, the state itself would have to maintain defence industries against such a contingency. At the source of liberal theory, therefore, there is this major concession to realism. It would be an obvious absurdity to allow deference to the principle of comparative advantage to lead to dependence on a potential enemy for the means of military survival. No one has ever successfully challenged this claim that the first duty of a state is to its citizens.

Once national defence was allowed to breach the purity of *laissez-faire* economics, there could be no logical objection to other concessions to nationalism providing it could be similarly demonstrated that the essential security of the community was at stake. In principle, the natural harmony of interests required free movement across state boundaries of all the factors of production including labour. By the beginning of the twentieth century, however, any pretence that the major industrial societies would maintain a free labour market had been abandoned. Mass unemployment was bound to confront the state, therefore, with a major political and moral problem, particularly once it had been demonstrated that a modern war could not be fought without military conscription and the creation of a war economy requiring the mobilisation of the civil population. If the democratic state had the right to compel men to sacrifice their lives for their country in war it could hardly treat them as a mere commodity in peace. The politicisation of the labour market, first through the introduction of immigration controls and then in response to the Great Depression, severely weakened the assumption that economic rationality could dispose of the problem of obligation except in the limiting case of war.

This assumption has proved far more difficult to dislodge at the international level. In turning against the orthodox support for Free Trade (his concern was to make practical proposals for solving Britain's unemployment problem) Keynes challenged not the ideal world of *laissez-faire* which, with modifications, he continued to support, but 'its tacit assumptions [which] are seldom or never satisfied, with the result that it cannot solve the economic problems of the actual world'.[8] It may be, as Joan Robinson maintains, that Keynes 'succeeded in bringing back the moral problem into economics by destroying the neo-classical reconciliation of private egoism and public service'[9] but he pulled his punches at the frontier. Since he did not challenge the ideal world of the liberal tradition, he had little to say about international as opposed to national obligations. For Adam Smith the state played a vital but purely regulative role. Keynes endowed it with positive functions designed to check the notoriously heartless and, as he believed, politically dangerous consequences of non-interventionist policies at the state level. 'But if our central controls succeed in establishing an aggregate volume of output corresponding to full employment as nearly as is practicable, the classical theory comes into its own again from this point onwards.'[10] His ideas for international reconstruction after 1945 were essentially aimed at creating an environment in which the state could meet its obligations to its own citizens; once that was achieved he was content to rely on the benevolence of the hidden hand in the wider international community.

As has often been pointed out Keynes was concerned to save liberal society from itself. To do this he sought to show that where resources were chronically underutilised it was necessary for the state itself to create demand. This in turn meant that in certain circumstances the legitimacy of economic nationalist, that is, protectionist, policies would have to be acknowledged. Since no international authority existed which could have taken responsibility for stimulating the world economy as a whole, and since the experience of the 1930s suggested that competitive economic nationalism was self-defeating, the practical and theoretical problem was now the same: how to protect the Western liberal order, not from a more attractive doctrine but from the compelling pressures of a self-destructive atavism. The problem in other words was how to achieve by management what the classical and neo-classical economists thought they had demonstrated by argument, the reconciliation of private, national and international interests.

II

To this end the economic philosophers joined forces with the diplomats. During the Second World War both the Atlantic Charter and the terms of the Lend Lease Agreement committed the British and American governments to the creation of a liberal international economy as an integral part of the wider postwar order. The purpose of this section is to sketch very briefly the strategy that was devised and secondly to evaluate the implicit theory of a community of interests on which it was based.

In the first instance the aim was to create the conditions of confidence in which international trade could expand through the maintenance of stable exchange rates between the major currencies. The emergence of the dollar exchange standard, which lasted until 1971, whereby the dollar was denominated in terms of gold at thirty-five dollars an ounce and other currencies in terms of the dollar, amounted in effect to an admission that the international monetary system would only work if the majority of governments accepted its operation as broadly fair. This they would only do of course first, so long as they wanted dollars for trading purposes and were satisfied that they represented an adequate store of value for reserve purposes, and secondly, providing they could adjust their own exchange rates when the existing system of parities threatened their commitment to full employment. The International Monetary Fund, which provided short-term balance of payments relief, and the consultations which took place under its auspices and, perhaps more importantly, beyond its reach between central banks, ensured the broad legitimacy of this arrangement.

On the basis of the monetary order GATT then sought to remove the national policies that distort trade through the reduction of tariffs and the abolition of quotas and export subsidies. Here again the intention was to create conditions under which the market mechanism could operate although, as in the monetary field, it was recognised that this could only be achieved through the creation of a trading regime which was considered fair to all parties; for this reason the General Agreement was constructed around the most favoured nation principle (m.f.n.), the minimum condition of reciprocal security under which states could be expected to liberalise their economies. So long as the major obstacles to the open international economy were perceived to lie with traditional protectionism, the GATT approach was well suited to the kind of technical negotiation required to overcome them. Every country operated a tariff and all could agree that, subject to certain safeguards, it was desirable that their overall level should be reduced.

During the 1960s, however, the assumption of a fundamental identity of interests which had underpinned this strategy gradually collapsed. In the monetary field the United States' allies first challenged a system which allowed the USA to maintain a seemingly permanent balance of payments deficit without having to confront the necessity of domestic adjustment, and then when the competitive position of some allies, notably Germany and Japan, improved dramatically, the United States accused them of refusing to share the burden of maintaining the liberal order by revaluing their currencies.

The position with regard to trade similarly exposed the fragility of the reconciliation of national and international interests that had been achieved by GATT. As industrial tariffs came down it became clear that governments were also pursuing protectionist policies by other means. But precisely because, as a recent report of the Trilateral Commission put it, 'their social and political importance and the character of the institutions with which they are implemented carry some of these policies beyond the reach of the conventional approach',[11] they threatened to undermine the m.f.n. principle as the basis of the commercial order. Voluntary restraint agreements, for example, the multifibre agreement, the purpose of which is to reduce the pressure for a return to protection by negotiating the rate of increase of low-priced imports, and the framing of codes of conduct to apply to such major instruments of industrial policy as domestic subsidies and public procurement, represent pragmatic attempts to reconcile competing obligations to citizens and to trading partners. Such efforts no doubt reveal a lingering commitment to managed liberalism but it is clearly a fairly weak commitment.

Why has it proved so difficult to realise the community of interests in practice? Some economists have attempted to answer this kind of question by analysing the concept of a public good. In *The Logic of Collective Action*, Mancur Olson challenged the conventional assumption that 'groups of individuals with common interests are expected to act on behalf of their common interests much as single individuals are often expected to act on behalf of their personal interests'.[12] On the contrary, he sought to demonstrate that even when members of a group would gain by acting to achieve their common interests, if they are rational and self-interested they will not do so. The basic explanation for this paradox lies in the nature of a public or collective good which is defined as one whose purchase cannot be made exclusive: in other words, those who do not pay for the good none the less cannot be prevented from consuming it. There is thus a conflict between the individual, whose rational aim is to maximise his interests at the least cost, and the interests of the group as a whole. This conflict can be resolved, according to Olson, in one of two ways: either the group can be coerced into meeting the cost of the good, as in the case of the state which invariably insists on compulsory taxation to cover the cost of fundamental services, or those who bear the cost of providing a public good can be rewarded by the provision of some separate, that is, exclusive, advantage as in the case where members of a professional association can obtain legal or financial assistance which would not be provided to non-members.

Two questions arise in any attempt to apply this line of reasoning to international economic relations. What is the identity of the group or groups with which we are concerned? And what is the nature of the public good which the group exists to provide? In the light of the attempt to manage the international economy since 1945 two answers to the first question suggest themselves. The group can be interpreted either exclusively or inclusively, in other words it can be taken to mean either those Western industrialised states which are members of the Atlantic Alliance and with some additions of OECD, or all states whose governments or citizens are involved in the international economy. As regards the nature of the collective good it can be given a determinate identity only in the most general terms, that is, the provision of economic security through an agreed regime to govern international economic relations.

From the exclusive perspective of the Western Alliance it is clear that an attempt was made to establish such a regime. Since the alliance was a voluntary association of states it was not possible to coerce them into bearing equal shares of the cost: while all could accept that monetary stability was a 'good', self-interest dictated that the United States, the strongest member of the alliance, should pay a disproportionate share of the cost in any case. Of course there were special incentives which were not on offer to the rest of the alliance, in particular the possibility of choosing the monetary system which suited them best. In 1945 the Americans were apprehensive that, in the face of the strong US economy, other countries would want to devalue. They, therefore, chose a fixed rate system to limit devaluation against the dollar and insisted upon a very high quota in the new IMF – at one point over 30 per cent.[13] But when the US perception of its own interest changed during the 1960s and its economic lead over its allies narrowed it still could not shift the burden of underwriting the international economic order on to its partners.

As a consequence the regime began to fall apart. Since 1971 there has been no formal international monetary order. Expert opinion on whether this has damaging consequences for the international economy is divided, although the attempt to create a European Monetary System suggests that in some parts of the Western Alliance interest in monetary stability persists. More important for the present discussion is the fact that the attempts to reform the wider monetary system have very largely failed, a failure which, in the absence of coercion or exclusive incentives, the theory of collective goods would lead one to expect.

The theory is less helpful, however, in explaining why the Western economic order does not disintegrate altogether, why, in other words, disputes over burden-sharing have not spilled over into open political conflict. Two obvious answers suggest themselves. The first is that, in the final analysis, the non-communist world is coerced into co-operation by the recognition of a common threat; the second that the inter-penetration of market economies has locked them into a system of no escape so that disputes over the justice of particular arrangements or over cost-sharing of joint policies are of only marginal significance; in the end governments will be forced to accommodate one another in order to survive. Maybe. But such accommodation, in mitigating the consequences of protectionism in intra-Western trade, may be also as much a function of a shared historical experience, a community of values and of similar social and economic structures as of interests. It seems probable, for example, that it is on the basis of these shared characteristics rather than as a consequence of mechanical rationality that habits of consultation and mutual economic surveillance have developed within OECD. Arguments about the rationality of burden-sharing may throw light on the difficulty of articulating a general interest within a specific group, but, like all rationalist arguments, they cannot satisfactorily explain why such groups come into existence or the point at which they will finally disintegrate. The Western community may be in disarray because of its inability to reconcile competing national and alliance interests but it palpably continues to exist.

The theory of public goods has to be stretched even further if the group is interpreted inclusively, that is, to include all states whose governments or citizens are involved in the international economy. Olson argues that 'in groups composed of members of greatly different size or interest in the collective good' there is a tendency towards an arbitrary sharing of the cost of provision. This is because 'once a smaller member has the amount of the collective good he gets free from the largest member, he has more than he would have purchased for himself' so that in such groups there is 'a surprising tendency for the "exploitation" of the great by the small', a possible explanation, he suggests, for the popularity of neutralism among smaller countries.[14] In this example security is the 'good', the cost of which is presumably borne disproportionately by one or other of the major alliance systems. This seems a most implausible explanation of neutralism, since it implies that the governments of small countries regard great power armaments as somehow providing them with security free of charge. A similar kind of argument, in the economic field, would imply that the benefits of the Western economic order are provided free to Third World countries, a view which may reflect official opinion in some Western governments but emphatically not that of their Southern counterparts many of whom evidently believe that it is they who are shouldering a disproportionate proportion of the costs of Western economic disorder.

The basic reason for the disenchantment of Third World governments with the Western international economy is well known. It arises from their contention that international economic security requires income redistribution. Like Bismarck before them, spokesmen for developing countries regularly point out that free trade is the natural (which in this context means nationalist) policy of the strongest power. In that the GATT is an instrument of classic liberal machinery the criticism is fair. Its underlying philosophy is both negative and procedural; the m.f.n. rule provides states with the assurance that in freely pursuing their own interest, they will not be preventing others from doing the same, but it has no redistributive implications.

After 1945 pressure for income redistribution was accommodated in industrial societies, wherever there was a government with the authority to carry through the necessary reforms. Indeed income redistribution was often the price which Western governments had to pay to secure the continued viability of the mixed economy and liberal polity.[15] And the external aspect of the liberal polity was the commitment to an open trading system. Over much of the Third World, however, the mixed economy, in the sense of the coexistence of private and public enterprise in 'modern' economic activities, did not exist; in such countries, moreover, the political objective of modernisation was generally held to imply economic diversification and the establishment of an industrial base. This required, at a minimum, increased earnings of foreign exchange (or some substitute for such earnings) to cover the cost of the necessary investment. Since it was only though their involvement in the world economy, as suppliers of raw materials and agricultural produce, that the money could be earned, from the start Third World governments argued for positive action programmes at the international level. The North–South conflict developed out of these demands for an international community based on purposive action rather than negative rules. It is a conflict not about who should pay for an agreed 'good' but about the principles of justice on which the international community should be based.

To summarise. In the first section I argued that liberal economists proposed a 'natural' reconciliation of private, national and international interests but that they also accepted that the state had a prior obligation to defend its citizens, an obligation which was subsequently reinterpreted and expanded by Keynes to include the pursuit of full employment policies. However, the contradiction between the idea of a natural or mechanical community of interests at the international level and the community of citizens whose rights and obligations were reflected in the institutions of civil society could only be resolved under conditions of peace. In the second section I suggested that, with this in mind, the Americans and their allies had attempted after 1945 to build into the reconstructed international order a system of liberal economic rules but that this attempt had failed to withstand conflicts of interests within the Western alliance and between North and South. Since an appeal to the rationality of providing for economic security by collective action is evidently insufficient to preserve the existing international order, it remains to ask whether deliberate attention to principles of justice in the international community may throw some light on our current economic discontents.

III

No doubt most governments could agree to an economic equivalent of Montesquieu's definition of the war compact: 'to do the most good in peace time and the least possible harm in war consistent with the defence of vital general interests'. This is the conventional morality of states. But the absolute priority given to state interests weakens any commitment to the conduct of economic relations according to principles which are accepted as both orderly and just where there is a perceived conflict between principles and interests. Since it is difficult to conceive of a definition of community which does not involve the idea of a common purpose or interests with priority over particular individual interests, it would seem to follow that there is no community of states. Since all governments also perceive their first duty to be towards their own citizens rather than to the citizens of other states or to mankind, on this view, it would also seem to follow that there is no prospect of the emergence of such a community.

If this conclusion is not fully plausible it is perhaps because the need for economic co-operation is so widely acknowledged. A willingness to co-operate in principle, however difficult it turns out to be in practice, is certainly evidence of some kind of shared community sentiment. Indeed, on the evidence of the huge investment of diplomatic effort in economic negotiation, it is not the possibility of a community of states which is at issue so much as its 'constitutional' arrangements. The debate is between the supporters of two kinds of community each of which rests on a different conception of justice. The confrontation of these two conceptions, roughly speaking the regulative and the purposive, the first of which conceives of justice in terms of deserts, the second in terms of need, is most marked in North–South relations and it is in this context that I shall consider it.

The Western conception is of an association of states, like-minded in that their governments accept that, however interventionist they may be at home, they lack both power and authority to set positive goals for the international economy as a whole. In these circumstances their joint interests can be approximated only by securing agreement on an essentially regulative order based on reciprocity and negative injunctions against discriminatory trading practices. It may reasonably be objected of course that the commitment to this order is itself a positive goal for the states which voluntarily endorse it. I shall return to this point shortly; for the moment it is important to note that Western governments, with the possible exception of France, have never committed themselves to a view of the international community which involved an obligation to engage in the positive direction of the world economy: the furthest they have been willing to go is consultation on national economic policies, for example, within OECD, with a view to minimising any damage to the interests of partner states. In the Western political tradition the acceptance of any wider obligation would require the prior creation of a civil society, and a world citizenship to which the global managers would be accountable.

Although the interests of Southern states often differ dramatically, they have been able to articulate a general interest in an international community based on the principle of distributive justice. Whether their specific demands rest on the case for reparations for past exploitation or, as in the Brandt Commission Report, on an appeal to long-run mutual interests with Northern states, the assumption is that, given political will in the North, the institutions of the international economy could be restructured to secure automatic income transfers and to provide Third World governments with a greater voice in global decision-making. The issue of accountability, let alone of citizenship, is generally avoided.

The significance of this omission can hardly be overstated for it explains the difference between those areas of North–South relations where it is possible to make 'progress' and those where it is not. The crucial distinction here is between an international economic order regulated by negative rules designed to ensure fair trading, for example, non-discrimination, and an association which exists to promote certain policies, for example, price enhancement or the management of world markets. The former does not, in principle, challenge the primacy of the state's obligation to its own citizens, the latter obviously does. In practice, of course, even the commitment to abide by fair trading rules may be difficult to maintain, for example, during periods of high unemployment. It was in recognition of this danger that exceptions to the m.f.n. rule were envisaged within GATT and that the IMF sought to shorten the duration and lessen the degree of disequilibria in the

balance of payments of its member countries, the aim being to enable
them to withstand nationalistic pressures for protection. It is in this
sense that it can justly be said that the rules of the liberal economic
order represent a common purpose of Western states.

Similar reasoning has governed official Western responses to Third
World demands. In so far as these have been entertained, for example,
in the granting of preferential access for Third World manufactured
exports or compensatory financing of the short-falls in their foreign
exchange earnings, this has been with the intention of enabling developing countries to stay within the broad rules of the open world trading
system; it has not been with a view to treating the community of states as
an enlarged form of civil society. For example, the eventual negotiation
within UNCTAD of the General Specialised Preference scheme could
be regarded as an extension of the 'infant industry' principle: it was no
good advocating industrialisation and export-led growth if the
industries, once established, were prevented from penetrating Western
markets. Such concessions in other words were designed to support the
liberal order, not to transform it.

It is sometimes argued that the successful challenge by OPEC to the
Western economic order has completely changed the political context
within which the international economy functions and that the Western
powers must now necessarily accommodate demands for structural
reform of the international economy in much the same way as the
middle classes were forced to accommodate the interests of the workers
once organised labour had successfully challenged the bourgeois state.
In other words the claim is that a reappraisal of the concept of justice on
which the community is based is a necessary consequence of a
successful demonstration of political power.

Both this claim and the analogy from which it is derived need to be
handled with circumspection. Two consequences of the 'oil revolution'
are matters of historical record. First, the sudden quadrupling of the oil
price in the middle 1970s powerfully reinforced inflationary pressures
throughout the industrial world and contributed to the world recession.
To this extent it no doubt also contributed to the further weakening of
Western commitments to the open world trading order. Secondly, the
crisis concentrated the attention of the industrial powers on their
varying dependencies on other raw materials produced in the Third
World. Faced with the need to secure supplies Western governments
engaged in wide-ranging discussions with the Third World governments as a token of their commitment to partnership. It was in this
changed climate that the EEC negotiated the STABEX mechanism, the
first international agreement which transfers resources to Third World
countries 'as of right', and that within UNCTAD, the industrial
countries finally agreed to the establishment of a Common Fund to help
finance commodity agreements.

For the purpose of the present discussion, however, it is more important to note what did not happen than what did. Despite pragmatic adjustments there was no major development in either economic or political thought in response to the energy crisis. The West did not convert to the Third World conception of community. In the case of the Common Fund, for example, agreement was only reached when the idea of using the institution as a redistributive mechanism was abandoned.[16] In other words the Western objective remains to make only those concessions which are consistent with the spirit of the liberal order and which will enable Third World countries to stay within it.

The attempt to force a radical reappraisal of the Western conception of the international community was bound to fail in that the domestic analogy on which it was based was in one crucial respect false. Democratic socialist parties were able to insist on positive reforms aimed at the redistribution of income because workers were also citizens. It is true that reform was seldom achieved without pressure but what was at stake was not merely the transfer of resources from rich to poor but the overall direction of government policy. Once this has been decided, for example, by extending the fundamental services of the state to include unemployment pay or free medical services, all citizens of whatever class or status remained subject to the law, the rights of membership of the community matched by corresponding obligations. Not only were the oil-producing states not in the same relation to Third World countries generally (the majority of whom suffered as a result of the rise in oil prices) as the early trade unions to the working class as a whole, but in the demands of resource transfers 'as of right' it was not clear what, if any, obligations were envisaged to match the new rights. In such circumstances the Brandt Commission's talk of, for example, a global development tax on armaments does not deserve to be taken seriously.

It would be wrong to conclude, however, on a negative note. All that has been claimed is that the necessary conditions for the reform of the international community on the basis of distributive justice do not at present exist. It does not follow that all considerations of justice must be excluded from economic relations between states. In any community disputes about justice tend to fall into one of two categories, disputes about desert and disputes about need. Within the conventional morality of states, for the reasons which I have discussed, disputes about desert can in principle be resolved whereas disputes about needs present a more intractable problem. A topical example may help to illustrate this point. The widely shared view that the debt problem of the developing countries is getting out of hand and that massive defaulting would have serious repercussions throughout the world economy suggests that the Western powers have an interest in trying to prevent it happening. One means available to them is to attempt to distinguish between the sources of disequilibrium which are beyond the control of deficit countries (for example, that part of their deficit which represents a counterpart of structural surpluses in the oil-producing and other countries) and those which are not (for example, excessive pressure of domestic demand). To the extent that economic expertise enables such a distinction to be made, there is clearly a case on grounds of desert for extending the facilities of the IMF, which were designed for this purpose, to cope with the problems beyond their control.[17] Even in this kind of case the difficulty of securing agreement is great; there is nothing to be gained, therefore, by compounding the difficulty through the introduction of the concept of need in circumstances where it cannot apply.

Will these circumstances inevitably change? It may be fairly argued that knowledge creates its own imperatives and that given our knowledge of the extent of world poverty and of the material degradation which much of mankind endures the conventional morality of states must yield to a genuinely cosmopolitan morality. Indeed, some international lawyers maintain that an international community based on the principle of distributive justice is already coming into existence as the result of a combination of Third World pressure and a growing appreciation of the necessity of co-operation in a world of finite resources.[18] That it should be brought into existence is also essentially the position adopted by Charles Beitz in a recent book which seeks to refine Rawls's theory of justice in its application to international relations.[19] Beitz argues that the extent of interdependence in the modern world lends support to the view of international economic relations as 'a global scheme of social co-operation' and, therefore, by analogy 'to a principle of global distributive justice similar to that which applies within domestic societies', that is, one under which social and economic arrangements would be to the benefit of the least advantaged.[20]

In working out his ideal theory of international distributive justice, Beitz scrupulously observes the problem of application in a non-ideal world but advocates none the less using mechanisms embedded in international instutions to effect redistributive transfers on the ground that these provide the best assurance, in the absence of a world authority, that the costs of redistribution will be shared fairly. The view offered in this chapter, on the other hand, would imply that an ideal theory of distributive justice cannot be translated even approximately into the non-ideal world of sovereign states without political agreement on the 'constitutional' arrangements of the community, arrangements which would necessarily include the acceptance of obligations as well as rights by all members. Without such matching of obligations to rights there can be absolutely no assurance not only that the rich will pay up but also that the governments of the Third World, the beneficiaries of any redistribution, will not misappropriate the funds. But Beitz is clearly correct in claiming that the most pressing issues in contemporary international theory are those which divide the morality of states from cosmopolitan morality, whether this is derived from Kantian philosophy or from some version of natural law. The challenges offered to the morality of states by these philosophies I leave to the chapters that follow.

NOTES: CHAPTER 7

1 Chapters 1 and 2.
2 Cf. Isaiah Berlin, 'The purpose of philosophy', in *Concepts and Categories* (Oxford: Oxford University Press, 1980), pp. 1–11.
3 Joan Robinson, *Economic Philosophy* (Harmondsworth: Penguin, 1962), p. 18.
4 On the relationship of Smith's 'natural liberty' to collaboration, see Joseph Cropsey, 'The invisible hand: moral and political considerations', *Political Philosophy and the Issues of Politics* (Chicago: University of Chicago Press, 1977), pp. 77–89.
5 Adam Smith, *Wealth of Nations*, Book 1, Vol. 1, ch. 4.
6 'Capitalism, war and internationalism in the thought of Richard Cobden', *British Journal of International Studies*, vol. 5, no. 3 (October 1979), pp. 229–47.
7 P. Straffa (ed.), *The Works of David Ricardo* (Cambridge: Cambridge University Press, 1951), Vol. 1, pp. 133–4.
8 J. M. Keynes, *The General Theory of Employment Interests and Money* (London: Macmillan, 1973), p., 378.
9 Joan Robinson, op. cit., p. 80.
10 J. M. Keynes, op. cit., p. 378.
11 John Pinder, Takashi Hosomi and William Diebold, *Industrial Policies and the International Economy*, Triangle Papers 19 (New York: The Trilateral Commission, 1979).
12 Mancur Olson, *The Logic of Collective Action* (Cambridge, Mass.: Harvard University Press, 1971), p. 1.
13 See Jeremy Morse, 'The dollar as a reserve currency', *International Affairs*, July 1979, pp. 359–66.
14 Mancur Olson, op. cit., pp. 35–6.
15 cf. Ernest Gellner, 'A social contract in search of an idiom: the demise of the Danegeld state', in *Spectacles and Predicaments* (Cambridge: Cambridge University Press, 1979), pp. 277–307.
16 For a discussion of the Southern and Western views of the Common Fund see Geoffrey Goodwin and James Mayall (eds), *A New International Commodity Regime* (London: Croom Helm, 1979).
17 For a similar argument using the same example see Dudley Seers, 'North-South: muddling morality and mutuality' and Sidney Dell, 'The world monetary order', in *Third World Quarterly*, vol. II, no. 4 (October 1980).
18 See, for example, Oscar Schachter, *Sharing the World's Resources* (New York: Columbia University Press, 1977).
19 Charles Beitz, *Political Theory and International Relations* (Princeton, NJ: Princeton University Press, 1979).
20 ibid., pp. 143–53.

Part Three
Alternative Positions

8
The Individual and International Relations

PETER F. BUTLER

Of the many ideas that have shaped men's understanding of international relations, three have been of particular importance: the individual person; the nation or state; and the more general community of mankind. Although these ideas have prompted attempts to identify levels of analysis or causality in an empirical sense,[1] our concern here is with moral understanding. By moral understanding I mean an appreciation of an aspect of life, such as international relations, which provides guidance as to how one ought to act, and how one may praise, blame, or otherwise assess actions and developments in a way that goes beyond mere empirical description.

The ideas of the individual, the state and the global community of mankind have each, at various times, played important roles in attempts morally to understand aspects of international relations. Condemnations of violations of human rights place the individual at the centre of moral concern. In the war crimes tribunals following the Second World War, it was held that the individual could not ignore his moral responsibilities as an individual towards other men; evident acts of great immorality could not be excused by an appeal to superior orders. Yet the state too has been given a moral identity. This is reflected, for example, in Article 2 of the Charter of the United Nations, which asserts that 'the Organization is based on the principle of the sovereign equality of all its Members' and requires members to refrain 'from the threat or use of force against the . . . political independence of any state'. Unlike other entities having legal personality, the treatment of individuals and states that accords with right has to take account of what individuals and states are intrinsically, and not merely refer to that which has been allowed them by a superior law-maker. Beyond the state, the idea of a global community of mankind has also determined judgements of a moral kind. Again in 'classical' writings on the law of nations the manifest similarity between men has prompted the thought that a great society of men exists, and that actions of individuals and states must, if they are to be right, recognise and reflect this great society. At the level of practice, we can note how both world wars became wars for civilisation and so derived additional legitimacy beyond that provided by *raison d'état*. Present uneasiness about global inequalities in the distribution of wealth and opportunity is surely related to the thought that no single community should tolerate such obvious injustices.

In this chapter, I wish to examine two approaches to the problem of ascribing proper relative weight to the claims of individual, state and global community. They are respectively those of writers in the secularised natural law tradition, notably Grotius and Vattel, on the one hand, and Kant's on the other. The Kantian approach is, I believe, a more satisfactory one, but to show why this might be so it is necessary first to examine its competitor.

I

That international relations can be regarded as a distinct subject for study testifies to the power of the idea of a distinct body of people united under a single government, as a basic political form. Of course, the history of Europe, and of the impact of Europe on the world, does not reflect perfectly the development of the idea of the nation-state as the main actor in international relations. In many ways the reality of past and present is very different from a world of distinct groupings of people, united under governments which enjoy control over demarcated and recognised territories. But the idea that the world is or should be regarded as a world of such entities has exerted great influence on efforts to bring order to international relations, whether through international law or specific international institutions. That we inhabit a world of states, that the leaders of states in some sense speak for their people and that through the ordering of relations between states mankind in general may best be served, are leading ideas in both thought and practice of international relations.

In practice, the impact of such ideas is seen in the ways in which actions which appear to infringe the autonomy of states are portrayed, by their perpetrators, as doing no such thing. The Israeli destruction of the Egyptian air force in 1967 was depicted as the justified pre-emption of a state that was itself about to launch an attack. The Soviet invasion of Czechoslovakia in 1968 was not seen as a repudiation of the idea of the autonomous state, but as a response to a more important requirement: the preservation of the socialist community. The seizure by the Iranians of the staff of the American Embassy in 1979 was to be excused because the staff were, allegedly, acting as spies rather than as legitimate diplomatic agents of their parent state. The Soviet invasion of Afghanistan in December 1979 was claimed to be no invasion at all, but a response to an invitation of the Afghan Government. The principle of state autonomy is honoured even in the breach.

This prominence in practice of the idea of the state is an echo of its importance in much speculation about the right ordering of relations among men, specifically in the work of many so-called 'classical' authors on the law of nations, and it is the interrelationships of the ideas of the individual, state and global community in that work that I now wish to explore.

For both Grotius and Vattel, the state is a natural entity, much more than the product of historical accident. Its natural necessity must be acknowledged once we recognise the unnaturalness of individuals living solitary, isolated existences. Grotius believed that 'among the traits characteristic of man is an impelling desire for society, that is, for the social life – not of any and every sort, but peaceful and organised according to the measure of his intelligence, with those who are of his own kind'.[2] For Grotius, even if man did not need the help of other men in order to survive as an individual, he would still be drawn to the society of other men. Vattel held that 'man is so formed by nature, that he cannot supply all his wants, but necessarily stands in need of the intercourse and assistance of his fellow creatures'.[3] Thus, while Grotius emphasised traits, and Vattel needs, both were agreed on the consonance between the nature of man and life within a society of men.

Having argued for the naturalness of life in society for men, both writers suggest that the best way to organise these social relations is through the institutions of a state. Grotius held that 'an association in which many fathers of families unite into a single people and state gives the greatest right to the corporate body over its members. This in fact is the most perfect society.'[4] Vattel argued that 'from the very design that induces a number of men to form a society which has its common interests, and which is to act in concert, it is necessary that there should be established a *Public Authority*, to order and direct what is to be done by each in relation to the end of the association'.[5]

The idea that life within a state is a prerequisite for the full realisation of human nature is a main determinant of Grotius's and Vattel's views on the rights and duties of men and their rulers. In general, by associating within a state, men agree to have decisions about how they ought to behave towards other men taken by a sovereign on their behalf. This does not mean that they agree completely to give up all rights to decide what is just themselves, however. Grotius held that 'if the authorities issue any order that is contrary to the law of nature or to the commandments of God, the order should not be carried out'.[6] Vattel saw 'no reason why the nation should not curb an insupportable tyrant . . . and withdraw itself from his obedience', since whenever a society 'confers the supreme and absolute government, without an express reserve, it is necessarily with the tacit reserve that the sovereign shall use it for the safety of the people, and not for their ruin'.[7] However, both writers were obviously aware that the right to resist or disobey a ruler should be exercised with caution. If injustice other than that of the extreme kind already mentioned were done or threatened by the sovereign, Grotius would have had us 'endure it rather than resist by force'.[8] Vattel, after an account of how the sovereign 'derives his authority from the nation',[9] argued that 'the nature of sovereignty, and the welfare of the state', will not permit citizens to oppose a prince whenever his commands appear to them unjust or prejudicial. This would be falling back into the state of nature, and rendering government impossible.'[10]

The idea that the state is a product of an act of association by individuals, who are impelled in that direction by their intrinsic natures or a sense of what serves their basic needs, has important implications for relations between states. Both Grotius and Vattel were fully aware of the horrors of conflict between states. One way of dealing intellectually with this would have been to argue that men should acknowledge one sovereign as supreme over the whole community of mankind. However, this path was not followed, for various reasons. Vattel, for example, argued that the needs of men were met sufficiently within particular states; there was not the same degree of necessity impelling men into a world-state as into a particular state.[11] Hence, for Vattel, the intellectual task was to supply, by an appeal to what was reasonable, a set of rules that should be followed in relations between states if individual states, and their human components, were to survive, realise their natures and meet their needs. The survival of individual states meant the same as the survival of the 'society of states', and the laws of nations were offered as rules to be followed by states if they were not so to disrupt the society of states as to make their own survival, which they were obliged to secure, precarious. Also, for Vattel, there were other mechanisms at work – notably the Balance of Power – which, arising from the structure of the system of states, helped secure the stability and preservation of the society of states.[12] Grotius too, by setting out those rules of natural law and more general rules based on custom and recognised authorities, sought to provide international relations with an orderly framework.

One of the major problems confronted by writers who sought to discover in reason a set of rules for the conduct of states was that of recognising when a breach of the law of nations had in fact taken place, and of determining what could be done about it. Grotius believed that war 'may rightfully be undertaken on behalf of any persons whatsoever', because of 'the mutual tie of kinship among men, which of itself affords sufficient ground for rendering assistance. "Men have been born to aid one another", says Seneca.'[13] Vattel, however, provided a powerful argument whose conclusion seems to be still accepted in much international practice, for example in the United States' public position that the war between Iran and Iraq that broke out in 1980 was not one in which the United States should intervene.

Vattel argued that states must be regarded as equal in a moral and legal sense, be they dwarfs or giants in fact.[14] After all, they were to be conceived of as having been created in the same way to meet the same needs. Thus it could not be supposed that any one state had been placed in a position from which it could judge the conduct of others. Within states, this right had been bestowed on the sovereign by the people. Between states, no such agreement had been made. Thus, it could not be supposed that any one state could make a judgement as to the rights and wrongs that had given rise to a war in which it was not involved. Wars were to be regarded as just on both sides. Indeed, this was seen as something that would improve the chances of peace and the survival of the society of states by preventing the expansion of a war.[15]

Something of the nature of the interrelationships between the three main concepts of individual, state and global community that is espoused within the 'classical' tradition should be plain from the above remarks on Grotius and Vattel. What man is, in terms of his inherent traits, or in terms of his physical needs, makes life within a state necessary and therefore natural. The requirement for social harmony at the level of the global community is met by the formulation of the laws of nations which, when followed, help preserve that larger community. In addition, for Grotius, the well-being of the global community was to be served by the acknowledgement of the right to make war on behalf of others, outside one's own state, who were suffering injury. For Vattel, who argues quite reasonably that the judgements needed to begin such actions presuppose a moral superiority on the part of the intervening state that it cannot be thought to possess, the needs of the global community are met by states staying uninvolved in the wars of others. The question of which of the two authors is closer to contemporary practice has been discussed at length elsewhere.[16] What is more important here is to notice some of the difficulties in arguments like Grotius's and Vattel's, which begin from an assessment of basic human needs or traits and then construct rules for international practice and institutions that most closely reflect those needs or traits. I wish to point out two problems in such attempts to determine right in international relations.

The first problem resides in the supposition that a moral quality such as rightness can be attributed to practices and mechanisms on the ground that they were or would have been agreed to by men who were conscious of their needs or impelled by basic traits such as sociability. I do not want to suggest that human traits and needs should not be reflected in human institutions, but only that no conclusions as to the rightness of such institutions can be drawn from the kinds of arguments – based on suppositions of traits and needs – that Grotius and Vattel employ. The laws of nations which Grotius and Vattel offer as means of maximising the possibility of human sociability or the meeting of human needs are, in Kantian terms, rules of skill or counsels of prudence, rather than moral commands. That is, they are descriptions of how we ought to behave in order to attain a previously chosen goal such as sociability. But this leaves us with the requirement to ask whether the goal is one that we have a moral duty to pursue. The rules set out by Grotius and Vattel have only a rightness conditional upon the assumed moral worth of the goal served by conformity to those rules.

The second problem becomes plain when we recognise that accounts, based on the idea of the original contract, of how men, sovereigns and states ought to behave, exhibit two modes of deriving conclusions on these matters. The first mode uses a supposition of what men, seeing that their basic traits or needs could not be met in a state of nature, would have agreed to in order to escape their difficulties. It is by this mode of derivation that the obligation of a government to act for the sake of its citizens, and of citizens to conform with their sovereign's understanding of what is necessary for the state's survival, are arrived at. The second mode of derivation involves considering what is entailed by the *idea* or concept of those organisations – the idea of the state, for example – that men are conceived of as having created in order to fulfil their natures and meet their needs. It is by this mode of derivation, for example, that Vattel arrives at the view that states not parties to a war have no right to judge between the combatants. Although Grotius held a different view, it is hard to deny that acceptance of a right of intervention would be inconsistent with the idea of states as morally and legally equal, an idea that is necessitated by an account of the creation of states by contract of their citizens. In other words, in the contract tradition – and notably in Vattel's account – the pursuit of interests, including the overriding interest in survival, can be seen to enmesh men in a web of conceptualisations which, in turn, determines the legitimacy of various kinds of behaviour.

An unsatisfactory aspect of such a mode of thinking as a guide to the determination of right action in international relations can be shown by positing a distinction between duty and obligation. Obligations derive from commitments entered into with others. Duties are unconditional moral requirements. One can, for example, hold that it is a duty to keep promises made; and also that one has a particular obligation to perform an action that was the subject of a particular agreement. But we can evidently imagine a situation where we might want to say that it is a duty not to enter into certain kinds of agreements because they are agreements to act in ways that are morally wrong. Now in Vattel's account, we find that by making particular agreements to enter into particular states, men have created a world in which right between states cannot be determined. A surrogate for the determination of true right is the acceptance of war as just on both sides, and of victory in war as the arbiter of right. But, as Kant points out, 'even the favourable issue of war in victory will not decide a matter of right'.[17] It would seem odd if we were to suppose that moral duty was fulfilled by an agreement to create a set of institutions if that agreement also implied an acceptance of the determination of many matters of right by such an obviously arbitrary means as superior strength.

II

The reason why those views are flawed which locate moral criteria in the supposed arrangements to which men might have assented in order to meet their needs and fulfil their natures, is because they do not explore the implications of an analysis of the concept of moral goodness for discussion about political right. Rather than beginning their investigations with an analysis of the concept of goodness, they first make other suggestions – about what men would have chosen in a state of nature – and only then seek to link these with notions of duty and right.

I want to suggest that Kant's awareness of such difficulties enabled him, in his writings on moral philosophy and politics, to lay the foundations of a much more powerful view of international morality.

Kant's moral theory differs from those of the authors I have discussed in that it starts from the concept of good, and seeks to discover what is entailed by our understanding of it. Chapter 1 of Kant's *Groundwork of the Metaphysic of Morals* opens with the famous assertion that 'it is impossible to conceive of anything at all in the world, or even out of it, which can be taken as good without qualification except a *good will*'. Qualities such as 'courage, resolution, and constancy of purpose' and talents such as 'intelligence, wit, judgement' that we normally assume to be characteristic of a good man can equally well be put to evil use if their possessor wills it.[18] Nor does goodness reside simply in the outcomes of actions. If it did, we would be unable to describe as good those efforts of a person which, through no fault of his own, failed to bring about any praiseworthy results; and that is plainly at variance with our understanding of the concept of moral goodness. Besides, like talents and qualities, outcomes can be used for evil purposes if it is so willed.

Goodness, then, is a quality of the will, and the way to a deeper understanding of goodness was, for Kant, to 'elucidate the concept of a will estimable in itself and good apart from any further end'.[19]

The possessor of a good will acts from a sense of duty. This is clear from the fact that we would be uncertain as to whether a man was good who derived personal benefit from actions which also seemed to produce general benefits. Only if we were sure that personal benefit was not the motive could we certainly judge the action as a good one. That is the same as saying that only if an action is done from duty can it certainly be regarded as good.

The next stage in the exploration of the nature of moral goodness is, therefore, to examine the notion of acting from duty. Kant saw that 'duty is the necessity to act out of reverence for the law'.[20] That is, to act because it is a law that one ought so to act, and to acknowledge the law as the source of one's action. The notion of reverence is very important here. One would not want to describe as dutiful the actions of someone who accidentally conformed to law, and dutifulness would not be the primary quality of actions that accorded with law because the actor feared the consequences of disobedience. But what is the content of this law? Its content cannot be determined by reference to the consequences that one might wish to emerge from adherence to law (the consequence of maximising the fulfilment of human needs, for example) for in that case we would be ascribing goodness to consequences in a way that Kant has already shown is at variance with the concept of goodness. Rather, it is 'only bare law for its own sake [that] can be an object of reverence and therewith a command'.[21] Kant then elaborates:

'But what kind of law can this be the thought of which, even without regard to the consequences expected from it, has to determine the will if this is to be called good absolutely and without qualification? Since I have robbed the will of every inducement that might arise for it as a consequence of obeying any particular law, nothing is left but the conformity of actions to universal law as such, and this alone must serve the will as principle. That is to say, I ought never to act except in such a way that I can also will *that my maxim should become a universal law.*'[22]

It is important to understand what Kant is doing here. He is exploring the concept of moral goodness, and forces us to admit that in many circumstances where we might want to call an action or person good, we must in fact admit the possibility of the presence of other characteristics that cast doubt on our original judgement. Moreover, by showing that we would not wish to deny the possibility of an action being properly describable as good which fails to bring about any consequences that might be thought good, we are led to recognise that goodness resides in the act of willing itself. Now any decision to act in a particular way can be regarded as the implementation of a maxim, or general principle of volition, by the actor. If I borrow money and promise to pay it back on a certain date, while intending only to repay it if there are not other things I would prefer to do with it when the time comes, then my particular action can be seen as an application of a maxim such as: keep your word only if it suits you. Whether such a maxim can produce moral action depends on whether it could be willed as a universal law. Plainly, the universalisation of this maxim would destroy the possibility of anyone giving their word on anything, and so actions based on such a maxim are immoral.

We can see, then, an important difference between the moral ideas which seem to underly what I have called 'classical' views on relations between states, and the Kantian position. For writers like Grotius and Vattel, the moral value of actions and institutions resides in the contribution they make to the fulfilment of human needs or in their consonance with such basic human traits as sociability. In other words, moral appraisals are made in the light of the consequences of actions and institutions for human beings. Kant, on the other hand, provides a powerful argument against being centrally concerned with consequences, and argues for a concern with the universalisability of the principles on which action is based. On balance, it seems to me that the Kantian view is more in accord with our understanding of the intrinsic possibilities of the concept of good. As Paton puts it: 'is not Kant saying the minimum that can be said about morality? A man is morally good, not as seeking to satisfy his own desires or to attain his own happiness (though he may do both of these things), but as seeking to obey a law valid for all men and to follow an objective standard not determined by his own desires.'[23]

Kant's general ideas about goodness play a major role in determining his views on how political life should be organised. Fundamental to his thought here is his formulation of what he calls the 'practical imperative' of morality: 'Act in such a way that you always treat humanity, whether in your own person or in the person of any other, never simply as a means, but always at the same time as an end.'[24] Kant's arguments in support of this view are complex, but the general point is, I believe, fairly simple. If moral action is action that results from reverence for a law that can be regarded as universal, then it can never be action which merely uses another person as a means to an end that is distinct from that person. To have reverence for a maxim that can be regarded as universal law for all beings capable of moral deliberation would surely be inconsistent with failing to respect as ends in themselves others who were similarly capable of revering universalisable maxims. To have respect for another entails never using him simply as a means to an end. Thus respect for the individual is fundamental in Kant's moral theory, and exerts a major influence on his account of how political arrangements should be organised. However, before summarising Kant's ideas in that direction, it is necessary to point out Kant's recognition of the necessary connection between freedom and the capacity to act morally.

Moral action is more than action merely in conformity with a universalisable maxim. The fact of mere conformity is simply contingent. A man is not moral simply because, by accident, his actions conform with such maxims. The goodness of an act can only result from the fact that he who has willed the action has recognised and revered the requirement to act morally. If an action is done, for example, on the orders of another, then no moral quality can be attributed to the actor, even if the act conforms with a universalisable maxim. And if such an action is done because the actor is forced to do it, or fears the consequences of not doing it, then that too has no moral significance; in such a case the action is simply a result of pressure, a mechanical or psychological determinance. A condition of moral action is that it be freely chosen action in conformity with universalisable maxims. How could we describe a man as good whose actions, even if they conformed with morality, were not the result of his own choice?

Given this understanding of the nature of moral action – action determined by reverence for self-imposed universal law – it is plainly impossible to make men moral by the use of law or other state machinery. It is however possible to describe a set of political arrangements which are in accord with the requirements of morality, arrangements that are right in an absolute sense, and to show how other arrangements are not at all consistent with those requirements.

To accord with morality, the state must reflect the supposition that it has been founded on a contract made amongst its people. However, this is not a contract made by people mutually to aid each other in pursuit of needs or happiness or other temporal advantage. Contract must be regarded as the basis of the state because only through a contract can individuals, conscious of the fact that their wills may clash and conflict in a state of nature, create a system of rules to direct their interaction in a way that preserves their freedom: 'according to the original contract, all (*omnes et singuli*) the people give up their external freedom in order to take it back immediately as members of a commonwealth . . . accordingly, we cannot say that a man has sacrificed in the state a part of his inborn external freedom for some particular purpose; rather, we must say that he has completely abandoned his wild, lawless freedom in order to find his whole freedom again undiminished in a lawful dependency, that is, in a juridical state of society, since this dependency comes from his own legislative will.'[25] The preservation of the possibility of freedom and hence of the possibility of moral action by individuals is thus the primary requirement of a political order, and that order is right only in so far as this is done.

The only kind of contract which will preserve the possibility of men acting in accordance with self-imposed universal laws is that which creates a republican constitution, 'the only enduring political constitution in which the law is autonomous and is not annexed to any particular person'.[26]

This view also has implications for our understanding of the arrangements that must exist at the global level if true right is to be a feature of international relations. Whereas Vattel seems to have been fairly content with a system of law that was imperfectly maintained by a combination of the reason and consciences of rulers and peoples, and by the systemic mechanism of the balance of power, Kant recognises that in the state of nature that exists among states, where what passes for right is determined in many cases by arbitrary strength, there is a requirement to move out of this condition. The rights that states are accepted as having in their present condition are 'merely provisional' and the condition is one 'that should be abandoned in favor of entering a lawful condition'.[27] Kant's understanding of the nature of moral action thus leads him to recognise the necessity of extending to the global level arrangements for men to prescribe laws to themselves. While the rational mode of ordering world society would be to establish a 'universal republic' Kant is aware that it would be ridiculous to expect existing states, jealous guardians of what they take to be their rights, to acquiesce in the loss of those rights. Thus a 'negative surrogate' is proposed, 'a Federation of the States averting war, subsisting in an external union, and always extending itself over the world'.[28]

Kant also provides us with some examples of aspects of the world as it exists that are inconsistent with his understanding of the requirements of morality. 'No state having an existence by itself – whether it be small or large – shall be acquirable by another state through inheritance, exchange, purchase or donation.'[29] Such a transfer would be quite at variance with the duty to treat humanity never simply as a means. The maintenance of standing armies is also at variance with that duty: 'for men to be hired for pay to kill or be killed, appears to imply the using of them as mere machines and instruments in the hand of another, although it be the State; and . . . this cannot be well reconciled with the right of humanity in our own person'.[30]

III

It may seem that a consideration of the rather abstract speculations of writers of the seventeenth and eighteenth centuries has little relevance to contemporary concerns. Certainly in the bulk of present-day academic work on international relations we find little attention paid to questions of the kind considered by Grotius, Vattel and Kant. The emphasis is rather on attaining empirical knowledge, obtained by varying degrees of scientific precision, of the causes of events. Game theory, models of foreign policy-making, theories of underdevelopment and of the nature of dependency, heuristic models of various kinds of international systems, are all attempts at explaining outcomes causally. As such, they no doubt have a use, but their application presupposes a choice of goal, and it is by means of its ability to show ways of considering the choice of overall goals that an examination of the authors I have discussed derives its value. The Kantian position, for example, which I have suggested accords much more closely with our concept of good, permits us to look more closely at proposals which are justified on the ground that they meet basic human needs. Global inequalities are not wrong because they prevent large numbers of people from attaining minimum standards of civilised existence in a material sense, but because they are at variance with the ability of individuals to become moral actors, regulating their lives according to self-imposed universal laws. Arguments about multinational corporations and other transnational entitities which are wholly or partially removed from law should not only be conducted in terms of the contribution of such entities to the fulfilment of human needs, but should also consider their effects on the potential for moral autonomy of individuals. Discussions of the contribution of a system of nuclear deterrence to global stability should take heed of the fact that in such a system, the individuals who comprise the civilian populations of states in a relationship of nuclear deterrence are being used, as hostages, by the deterring states.

However, the moral dimension of international relations that is manifested by a consideration of the Kantian position should not be taken as an easy guide for conduct. Even in moving from a situation where the rights of men and nations are to be regarded as merely provisional, there is a requirement that individuals be respected as ends in themselves, that some not be used as means to the attainment of ends thought to be generally desirable. The progress towards a moral order in international relations must be by a gradual extension of the province of law understood as the mechanism by which men prescribe duties to themselves. To investigate, advocate and explain ways in which this can be achieved without destroying the albeit imperfect present bases of stability is surely at least as important as the pursuit of an understanding of the empirical causes of events. Indeed, without the former activity, the latter is little more than mere curiosity.

NOTES: CHAPTER 8

1   For example, in J. David Singer, 'The level-of-analysis problem in international relations', in Klaus Knorr and Sidney Verba (eds), *The International System:*

Theoretical Essays (Princeton, NJ: Princeton University Press, 1961), pp. 77–92.

2 Hugo Grotius, *The Law of War and Peace*, trans. Francis W. Kelsey (New York: Bobbs-Merrill, a reprinted edition of the Carnegie Classics edition of 1925), Prolegomena, section 6.

3 Emeric de Vattel, *The Law of Nations or Principles of the Law of Nature applied to the Conduct and Affairs of Nations and Sovereigns*, ed. Joseph Chitty (London: Sweet & Maxwell, 1834), Preface, p. XIV.

4 Grotius, op. cit., Book II, Chapter V, section XXIII.

5 Vattel, op. cit., Book I, Chapter I, section 1.

6 Grotius, I, IV, I.

7 Vattel, I, IV, 51.

8 Grotius, I, IV, I.

9 Vattel, I, IV, 45.

10 Vattel, I, X, 54.

11 Vattel, Preface, p. XIV.

12 Vattel, III, III, 47.

13 Grotius, II, XXV, VI.

14 Vattel, Preliminaries, 18.

15 Vattel, III, XII, 190.

16 For example, in Peter Pavel Remec, *The Position of the Individual in International Law according to Grotius and Vattel* (The Hague: Nijhoff, 1960) and in Hedley Bull, 'The Grotian conception of international society', in Herbert Butterfield and Martin Wight (eds), *Diplomatic Investigations* (London: Allen & Unwin, 1966), pp. 51–73.

17 Immanuel Kant, 'Perpetual peace: a philosophical essay', in M. G. Forsyth, H. M. A. Keens-Soper and P. Savigear (eds), *The Theory of International Relations* (London: Allen & Unwin, 1970), p. 212. The translation is W. Hastie's. 'Perpetual peace' appeared in 1795.

18 Kant, *Groundwork of the Metaphysic of Morals*, in H. J. Paton, *The Moral Law* (London: Hutchinson, 1948), p. 59.

19 Paton, p. 62.

20 Paton, p. 66.

21 Paton, p. 66.

22 Paton, p. 67.

23 Paton, p. 22.

24 Paton, p. 91.

25 Kant, *The Metaphysical Elements of Justice*, translated by John Ladd (New York: Bobbs-Merrill, the Library of Liberal Arts), p. 80.

26 Ladd, p. 112.

27 Ladd, p. 123.

28 Kant, 'Perpetual peace', in Forsyth *et al.*, p. 214.

29 Forsyth *et al.*, p. 201.

30 Forsyth *et al.*, p. 202.

9

Human Rights and International Community

ZDENEK KAVAN

International concern with human rights originated in Europe in the nineteenth century. Before the Second World War attention was concentrated on three issues, slavery, the humanitarian law of war and the protection of minorities. Several international agreements resulted. The practice of slavery was condemned at the Congress of Vienna in 1815 and the Anti-Slavery Act signed at the Brussels Conference of 1890. International concern with the conduct of war led to the Geneva Convention of 1864 and the Hague Conventions of 1899 and 1907; with the protection of minorities to the Treaty of Berlin of 1878 and the minorities treaties following the 1919 Peace Settlement.

The Second World War and the experience of Nazism and Fascism provided both an impetus for continued action on human rights and widened the area of concern. The United Nations Charter pledged the member states to 'cooperate in promoting respect for human rights and fundamental freedom for all' (Article 1) and declared that the UN shall promote 'universal respect for, and observance of, human rights and fundamental freedoms for all without distinction as to race, sex, language and religion' (Article 55). The Universal Declaration of Human Rights was adopted by the General Assembly of the UN on 10 December 1948. Although it does not impose legal obligations on the states, its declared aim was to provide 'a common standard for achievement for all peoples and all nations'. The Declaration on Colonialism in 1960 reaffirmed the commitment to both the human rights provisions of the UN Charter and the Universal Declaration, as did the Declaration on the Elimination of Racial Discrimination. Covenants on both Political and Civil Rights and on Economic, Social and Cultural Rights were approved by the General Assembly in 1966. European and American regional conventions have also been concluded. At the European Security Conference, which was held in

Helsinki in 1975, human rights were formally linked with *détente*. Since then official condemnations of various regimes for their human rights record have proliferated.

At first sight all this activity might be taken to indicate that there is a widespread international value consensus about what constitutes human rights and that a comprehensive picture of 'good government', proper relations between states and between men in general could be derived from these agreements and provisions. The issue is unfortunately more complicated. There are differing interpretations of human rights and the international concern itself has been justified and advocated on many different grounds ranging from those of national security to those of universal morality. This chapter will examine the major positions on human rights and then try to assess why international concern with these rights has become relatively so widespread and what this development tells us about the nature of the international community. Before turning to these questions, however, it is necessary to clarify the concept of international community itself.

I

'Community' is used here as interchangeable with 'society'. Although it is possible to make clear distinctions between the two concepts it is not necessary for the purposes of this chapter. 'Community' is interpreted as implying a structured pattern of interactions between men, and an acceptance of rules of behaviour by them based on shared perceptions of common values and interests. It must be noted that not all structured patterns of behaviour imply shared interests and values.

The two central arguments about international community question its existence and its membership. The argument denying the existence of international community is centred on the absence of central authority. This argument stresses the existence of a diversity of cultures in the world, the relative self-sufficiency of the state or region, and the conflictual as against consensual nature of international politics. If any rules of conduct are actually observed at any stage these are claimed to be the outcome of a temporary coincidence of interests. The lack of enforcement ability makes it unlikely that such rules will persist beyond this coincidence.

The arguments claiming the existence of international community emphasise the existence of agreements on certain rules of conduct that persist over time, such as the rules of diplomacy. Those who hold this view also point to the increased volume of interactions across national boundaries, and claim that the relative self-sufficiency of the state, if it ever existed, is long gone. Economic well-being as well as security, it is claimed, now require international co-operation. Although there is not a generally recognised central authority, there is a growing body of international law, institutions and practices that provide the basis of international order.

International community can be seen as consisting of states and possibly other group entities, or of individuals, or both. International law, on the whole, does not accept individuals as members of international community, at least it does not grant them the status of international legal subjects. On the other hand, international concern with human rights implies that individuals are the ultimate members of international community. As Westlake put it, 'the society of states . . . is the most comprehensive form of society among men, but it is among men that it exists. States are its immediate, men its ultimate members. The duties and rights of states are only the duties and rights of the men who compose them.'[1]

II

On this view agreement on human rights is clearly a crucial test for any international community. As I have already noted, however, there are different conceptions of human rights which are rooted in different political theories and cultures and which are used to justify different types of society and institutions. It is beyond the scope of this chapter to examine them all comprehensively. Instead my purpose is to shed some light on those conceptions that have a particular significance in the current international debate on human rights. I shall proceed by making four distinctions which often arise in the course of the debate before analysing them in the context of the theories within which the alternative interpretations and positions are advanced and justified.

(a) Universal vs Positive Rights
Universal rights are seen as rights that human beings have in virtue of whatever characteristics they have that are both specifically and universally human. They have these rights 'irrespective of nationality, religion, citizenship, marital status, occupation, income and other social and cultural characteristics, and also irrespective of sex'. It is claimed that these rights 'cannot merely be positive legal rights because people have them whether or not they have been enacted into positive law'.[2]

Positive rights, on the other hand, are derived from the state. Those who define human rights as positive rights, that is, rights which reflect the relationship between the state and its citizens, deny that there is any 'element in them which could be inferred from natural law, existing prior to the state'.[3]

(b) Individual vs Collective Rights
Individual rights belong to individual men only whereas collective

rights are claimed to belong to particular groups. The supporters of the latter often go on to claim that the liberty and rights of the individual can only be realised if the rights of the group to which he is deemed to belong are guaranteed first.

(c) 'Old' vs 'New' Rights

'Old' human rights were mainly political and civil rights and were centred on the notion of freedom. They defined the relationship between the individual and society and their primary function was to protect the individual against any arbitrariness of governments. They were the rights of recipience, that is, rights 'against someone else, rights to receive something from him, even if the something is simply the facility of being left alone',[4] which imposed negative obligations of non-interference on others.

'New' human rights include economic and social rights and are based on the notion of human needs. They impose 'positive obligations on others – to provide [the individual] with something which he could not achieve by himself'.[5] The advocates of these rights usually have a conception of liberty which goes beyond the notion of absence of restraint, of non-interference, and involves the ability to do something, to have a real opportunity to act on the basis of the material requirements of that action.

The two main justificatory theories within which these alternative conceptions are employed are liberalism and Marxist socialism. The liberal position on human rights is usually associated with the Western democracies. It evolved from the natural law tradition and was given its first coherent formulation by Locke. Locke derived natural rights from natural law (that is, reason) which established not only rights but their limitations and corresponding obligations ('no one ought to harm another in his life, health, liberty, or possessions'). These rights are equal as there is a natural equality of men, of their needs and capacities. Locke deduced three basic natural rights – a right to life, a right to liberty and a right to property. It is this last right that has attracted most criticism. Locke's critics have argued that this right supports and expresses man's selfishness and greed and undermines the claim of equality of men and of their natural rights. This is particularly so if the Lockean right to property is interpreted as being unlimited and based on the utilitarian argument about productivity. Even if the right to property is interpreted as being limited by the consideration of not depriving other men of the means of susbistence, it is difficult to see how this right could be realised in a way that would cater for both the requirement of equality and man's natural 'desire of having more than he needs'.[6]

The contemporary exponents of the liberal doctrines of human rights disagree on many issues but tend to agree that human rights are universal moral rights, that is, they belong to all men in all situations, and that they belong to them as individuals. They also emphasise the primacy of political and civil rights. Cranston, for instance, argues that economic and social rights cannot be considered to be human rights at all on the basis of the tests of paramount importance and practicability.[7] Raphael, on the other hand, accepts economic and social rights as universal rights but assigns them a weaker sense by asserting that they are claims that belong to all men but are claims against some men only (the state).[8] The emphasis thus tends to be on political liberty and equality, and a certain separation of the political sphere from the economic is assumed.

In turning to Marxist conceptions of human rights it is necessary to make a distinction between Marxism as derived from the thought of Karl Marx and Marxism as the official ideology of the Soviet Union. Although the former is more interesting and coherent, the latter is more relevant to the current international debate and practice of human rights.

Marx's position on human rights and his critique of the liberal position is based on his conception of human freedom as emancipation. He criticised the traditional conception of human rights and the right to freedom in particular for being based 'not on the union of man with man, but on the separation of man from man. It is the right to this separation, the right of the limited individual who is limited to himself. The practical application of the right of man to freedom is the right of man to private property' which is 'the right to enjoy his possessions and dispose of the same arbitrarily, without regard for other men, independently from society, the right of selfishness . . . It leads man to see in other men not the realization but the limitation of this freedom.'[9] The bourgeois political revolution, and the political emancipation it secured, separated civil society from the state, man from the citizen. Political freedom and its corollary, the equality of citizens before the law, is thus only partial emancipation and does not in itself lead to human liberty. It is based on a faulty assumption on the part of the bourgeois class that 'the whole of society is in the same situation as this class, that it possesses, or can easily acquire, for example, money and education'.[10] It is only in a classless society where the differences between civil society and the state are dissolved, where man can satisfy his needs and realise his potential, that true human emancipation can exist.

Marx's conception of human nature is also quite important here. It is often assumed, by non-Marxists especially, that Marx denied the existence of ahistorical human nature and saw men merely as social and historical products. Careful reading of Marx's earlier works in particular, however, leads to the conclusion that there is an underlying conception of human nature which is seen as the essence of man, his 'species-character', 'that which is universally human, and which is realized in the process of history by man through his productive activity'.[11] A distinction can thus be made between a general human nature and its specific manifestations in different cultures and historical stages. His recognition of the constancy of certain human drives and needs as against those that are rooted in specific social structures suggests that, in a fundamental sense, Marx was not a relativist and that the divide between his own thought and the natural law tradition is not altogether irreconcilable.

Marx's followers, as indeed his critics, have interpreted his ideas in many different ways ranging from economic determinism to complex interactionism. These differences tend to be reflected in attitudes to human rights and political rights in particular. The determinists pay little attention to political and civil rights which they see as determined by the material base. The Marxist humanists, on the other hand, who regard alienation as the central concept of Marxist thought, recognise the importance of political freedom and the progressive nature of political and civil rights in the present historical epoch.

In the Soviet bloc human rights in socialist societies are seen as being different from human rights under capitalism. They are perceived as reflecting the relationship between the citizen and the state where both accept duties which limit and define these rights. Thus human rights have a somewhat collectivist nature. One of Hungary's legal theorists puts it clearly: 'it is not the function of citizens' rights (and duties) in the socialist state and legal system to give birth directly to individual rights . . . citizens' rights are not devoid of individual features, but is is not their essence'.[12]

Indeed, the individual can easily disappear from the equation altogether so that violations of the rights of particular individuals tend to be seen as unimportant anomalies provided that his rights are embodied in the constitution, and general practice reflects the desired organisation of the collective and the will of the working class. If freedom is recognised necessity, a condition which involves working in or towards a particular social organisation in close collaboration with other men in the interests of the people, then freedom to dissent, for example, can be contradictory. The Soviet Minister of Justice explained the official interpretation as follows: 'Our laws lay down restrictions [on the right of holding opinion] which are necessary for protecting the working people's interests, and provide for penalties whenever these restrictions are violated.'[13] As the interest of the working men is determined by the party and the party rules the state, dissent from the party often ends as a 'threat to the interests of the working men'.

Within the Soviet bloc, therefore, political and civil rights are generally seen as being of secondary importance in relation to social and economic rights. To quote the Soviet Minister of Justice again, 'the whole problem of human rights cannot be limited to [the individual's rights and freedoms] alone while avoiding the question of social and economic rights, which bear on the material foundations of human life . . . All the other human rights and freedoms can be made real only on the basis of these social and economic rights.'[14]

One other justificatory position, the nationalist, is of interest here. In *The Duties of Man* Mazzini wrote: 'Without country you have neither name, token, voice, nor rights, no admissions as brothers into the fellowship of the peoples. You are the bastards of humanity . . . Do not beguile yourselves with the hope of emancipation from unjust social conditions if you do not first conquer a country for yourselves.'[15] The liberty of the individual is assumed to be dependent on the liberty of his nation or country. This sentiment found an expression in the principle of the right of nations to self-determination, a principle which has been legitimised in the postwar international agreements on human rights.

The enormous problems that this right involves are beyond the scope of this chapter. Suffice to say that the notion that nationality defines and exhausts human nature is dubious and that there are notorious difficulties in agreeing on unambiguous and applicable criteria for defining a nation and in applying the right to self-determination in case of conflicting claims. It is, however, worth noting that from the whole range of internationally agreed human rights this one has the greatest weight (in terms of general acceptance and impact) in contemporary international relations.

III

As I noted at the outset many international agreements on human rights have been concluded particularly since the Second World War. Concern with the safeguarding of human rights regionally and globally exercises foreign ministries, various international organisations – governmental and non-governmental, voluntary groups and individuals. Seemingly an enormous progress towards the globalisation of human rights enforcement has been made. The following problems, however, should be noted.

(a) Interpretation
As we have seen, conceptions of human rights differ. An agreement on a particular formulation of a resolution, declaration, or convention on human rights does not necessarily imply an agreement on their meaning. A neat formulation can in fact obscure the existence of a real conflict of conceptions. When this is the case, interpretations are likely to differ widely.

(b) Applicability

Most international agreements on human rights have been based on Western notions, whether liberal or socialist, and these 'may not be successfully applicable to non-Western areas for several reasons, ideological differences whereby economic rights are given priority over individual civil and political rights, and cultural differences whereby the philosophic underpinnings defining human nature and the relationship of individuals to others and society are markedly at variance with Western individualism'.[16] The ideological constraint on implementation can be detected from the argument of some political leaders in Third World countries who subordinate political rights to the economic requirements of development. Islam provides an example of a cultural constraint on implementation. Islam views materialism as detrimental to human dignity and the Western emphasis on freedom from external restraint is alien to it. Personal freedom is inner freedom realised through the seeking of God.[17] The course of the Islamic revolution in Iran indicates not only that there may be a tension between modernisation and Islam but also that the concept of human rights in general, whether priority is given to the political or economic rights of man, is of no concern to the Islamic revolutionaries. It should be noted in this context that rights are not necessary for the definition of the relationship between the individual and society.

(c) Enforcement

Some international agreements on human rights are only declaratory. The Universal Declaration of Human Rights, for example, did not establish contractual obligations between states; rather it was designed to establish common standards and principles. The International Covenant on Economic, Social and Cultural Rights is simply programmatic. Article 2 pledges the states to undertake 'to take steps, individually and through international assistance and cooperation, especially economic and technical, to the maximization of available resources, with a view to achieving progressively the full realization of the rights recognized in the present covenant'.[18] Even when the agreement is immediately enforceable, such as the International Covenant on Political and Civil Rights, the enforcement takes the form of reporting and depends on the pressure of the world public opinion.

One of the crucial problems is whether it is possible to reconcile international concern with human rights with the principles of state sovereignty and non-intervention. The tension is expressed in the UN Charter where Articles 55 and 56 pledge the member states 'to take joint and separate action in cooperation with the organization' for the achievement of universal respect for human rights while Article 2 (7) expressly prohibits interference in internal affairs in matters which are essentially within the domestic jurisdiction of any state. Current international practice seems to be weighted in favour of the principle of sovereignty. It is not surprising that only a very small number of states have signed and ratified the Optional Protocol of the International Covenant on Political and Civil Rights which permits petitions and communications from individuals to the Human Rights Committee on grounds of violations by their own state of any right contained in the Covenant.[19]

(d) Political Usage
Not only are different conceptions of human rights rooted in different political theories, but the realisation of a particular conception internationally is also not the main aim of governments. National security, the preservation of a particular social order and the securing of a favourable distribution of resources usually takes precedence. Inconsistencies of treatment are thus bound to occur. Furthermore, human rights can be advocated by particular governments for purposes other than the maximisation of these rights in the global arena. They can be utilised as a propaganda weapon for the purpose of unifying people at home and of causing internal difficulties as well as a loss of international prestige for an opposing state. Thus President Carter's well-publicised criticism of the Soviet treatment of dissidents was not always matched in its vigour when he addressed himself to the gross violation of human rights in some of the US client states in Latin America. In the absence of mutual trust, selectivity and inconsistency of treatment is bound to be interpreted as an expression of ulterior motives rather than universalist concern.

IV

Each of these four problems considered above has proved notoriously intractable. It remains to ask two questions: first, why none the less the protection of human rights has been progressively internationalised since 1945, and second, whether, despite the problems of interpretation and application, progress towards a greater degree of consensus is possible in the future. As regards the first of these questions the major historical reasons for internationalisation seem to be the following:

(1) The experience of Nazism led to a widely held belief that internal oppression leads to aggressive foreign policies and thus to a threat to international peace and security. This belief was common to West and East but it was not based on a shared view of what constitutes internal oppression. Thus a Hungarian theorist could state: 'The horrors of the Second World War, the ravages of Fascism were accepted as adequate evidence that Fascism combined overtly the annihilation of human rights within the state with oppressive tendencies directed against the

existence of other nations, and the wholesale contempt of the right of self-determination of the peoples. History thus proves that there was a close relationship between the preservation of international peace and security and the safeguard of the right of self-determination of the peoples and of human rights.'[20] He was evidently under no compulsion, however, to apply a similar analysis to Stalin's Russia.

(2) The volume of interactions across national boundaries has increased enormously and has had some cross-cultural impact. The globalisation of the previously European international system, which has accompanied this development, has in turn involved the spread of Western, including Marxist, ideas and theories.

(3) The state has been losing its relative self-sufficiency both in the security and economic spheres. The growing awareness of the existence of the world economy, interdependence and of vast inequalities of wealth strengthen the clamour for a more equitable distribution of resources on the part of the poorer nations. Claims for economic and social rights feature prominently in this campaign.

If the international concern with human rights shows this tendency towards the universalisation of values and the recognition of the existence of a global community of men, it also shows its current limitations. On the positive side some minimalist generalisations can be offered.

(1) In spite of the cultural and ideological diversity most states now subscribe officially to some doctrine of human rights.

(2) There are international agreements on human rights and there is a general consensus that international concern with human rights is legitimate. Governments proceed on the basis of a recognition that human rights have a universal popular appeal.

(3) Despite divergent conceptions, some minimal consensus can be inferred from these agreements, namely, that gross violations of human rights constitute a basis for the legitimisation of intervention – provided that it can be demonstrated that the violations in question pose a threat to international peace; and that there should be no arbitrary discrimination against the individual. In practice even the censensus on this latter point is quite minimal, as the argument as to what constitutes arbitrary treatment in specific conditions can differ quite widely.

(4) The activities of organisations such as the Amnesty International have successfully mobilised public opinion and in certain cases succeeded in pressurising a government into concessions.

On the negative side on the other hand are the following:

(1) The states still dominate this issue and ensure that sovereignty takes precedence.

(2) The divergence of views of human rights between the leaders of East and West is so great that there is little chance of significant progress in the near future. The Soviet government's view of human

rights as positive rights granted by the state which reflect a particular socio-economic organisation and express the interest of the working people as defined by the party, has little in common with the liberal concept of fundamental and natural rights. In such circumstances little fruitful debate is possible and mutual criticisms over human rights violations are likely to increase international tensions. This will be even more likely if governments persist in using human rights issues to gain political advantage.

In such circumstances the answer to the second question, whether progress is possible towards a greater degree of consensus on the conception and practice of human rights, is almost bound to be negative. In principle, however, this need not be the case. In the East–West context a more constructive dialogue between Marxists and non-Marxists is conceivable. The humanists on both sides could agree to several propositions such as that man should be treated as an end in himself; that his dignity is crucial to his humanity; that he has certain needs of which some are constant and some historically relative. Specific rights could then be derived from these propositions taking into account the specific historical conditions. Rights based on needs would be linked with obligations and thus provide a more comprehensive normative framework for the international community. In practice, the chances of humanists appearing in positions of authority on both sides are unhappily slim.

In the North–South context the issue is even more difficult due to the greater cultural divide and the greater disparity of socio-economic conditions. Economic rights based on human needs and linked with obligations on the part of the affluent would require a significant reorganisation of the world economy and reallocation of resources, and that is at present unlikely. Fundamental rights which exist prior to and are not related to obligations are unlikely to have a very profound impact in the South.

The conclusion is therefore pessimistic. Rapid progress in the international safeguarding and implementation of human rights is unlikely. If anything the issue is likely to generate more tension than harmony.

NOTES: CHAPTER 9

1 John Westlake, *Principles of International Law*, quoted in H. Butterfield and M. Wight (eds), *Diplomatic Investigations* (London: Allen & Unwin, 1966) p. 102.
2 A. J. M. Milne, 'The idea of human rights', in F. E. Dowrick (ed.), *Human Rights, Problems, Perspectives and texts* (Durham: Durham University Press, 1979) p. 23.
3 I. Szabo in J. Halasz (ed.), *Socialist Concept of Human Rights* (Budapest: Akademiai Kiado, 1966), p. 34.

4 D. D. Raphael, 'Human rights, old and new', in D. D. Raphael (ed.), *Political Theory and the Rights of Man* (London: Macmillan, 1967), p. 56.

5 ibid., p. 60.

6 C. B. Macpherson, 'Natural rights in Hobbes and Locke', in Raphael, op. cit., p. 8.

7 M. Cranston: 'Human rights, real and supposed', in Raphael, op. cit., p. 50.

8 D. D. Raphael, op. cit., p. 65.

9 K. Marx, 'On the Jewish Question', in D. McLellan (ed.), *K. Marx – Early Texts* (London: Blackwell, 1971), p. 103.

10 ibid., p. 93.

11 E. Fromm, *Marx's Concept of Man* (New York: Frederick Ungar, 1961), p. 34.

12 I. Szabo, op. cit., p. 73.

13 V. Terebilov, 'In defence of human rights', *World Marxist Review*, vol. 22, no. 7, p. 108.

14 ibid., p. 110.

15 G. Mazzini, *The Duties of Man* (London: Dent, Everyman edn, 1907), p. 53.

16 A. Pollis and P. Schwab, *Human Rights – Cultural and Ideological Perspectives* (New York: Praeger, 1979), p. 1.

17 A. A. Said, 'Human rights in Islamic perspectives', in Pollis and Schwab, op. cit., pp. 91–4.

18 A. H. Robertson, *Human Rights in the World* (Manchester: Manchester University Press, 1972), p. 35.

19 Ian Brownlie (ed.), *Basic Documents on Human Rights* (London: Clarendon Press, 1981), p. 146. The optional protocol entered into force on 23 March 1976 and twenty-three states have so far become parties to it.

20 Hanna Bakov, 'Human rights and international law', in Halasz, op. cit., p. 276.

10
A Community of Mankind

MICHAEL DONELAN

The business of foreign policy seems at first sight to consist solely of day-to-day decisions on issues as they emerge. Yet each decision, apparently based only on the facts of the matter, is influenced by ideas. There may be an overall strategy of the country's affairs. There will at least be a general climate of opinion about the situation of the country in its region and in the world and about what the overall problems facing it are. There will be, most profoundly and most permanently, a public philosophy about the nature of international politics and about dealing with other countries. All this influences day-to-day decisions. There is thus a continual need in foreign policy to debate the true shape of the overall problems and to reformulate the public philosophy in keeping with the times.

Over the past ten years, a novel view of the problems facing all countries and of the public attitudes appropriate to handling them has achieved a certain influence. Men, it is said, must first of all grasp that the problems are more radical than ever before in human history and so are the changes needed in attitudes. Beneath all the traditional comings and goings of the 150 governments of the world on their conventional concerns lie problems of an unparalleled magnitude and urgency. It is imperative that we shake off traditional perspectives and habits, resist the massive organisational inertia that forces our affairs into conventional channels, break out to a real grasp of these problems and adopt the new public attitudes that they demand.

We must first see clearly the fact, dulled by repetition, that the long history of growth of human weapons of destruction has in our time made a qualitative change. Certain countries, a growing number, now have the capacity to destroy not merely their enemies but all life on earth. The increasing indiscriminacy of weapons in the earlier part of this century has now taken a leap to total indiscriminacy. The countries thus armed are now by a supreme paradox describable in the phrase they once reserved for outlaws, 'hostes humani generis'. While the governments of these countries continue to come and go in the old manner about the vast bureaucratic business of national defence budgets, regional military alliances and international arms control negotiations, the clamant fact is that they possess what no one but a lunatic would think of possessing, arsenals of such a size, not just on land, not just on land and sea, but on land, sea and in the air, as to be capable of destroying the whole world, not just once but many times over; and that possessed as they still are by the old public attitudes, they show no signs whatever of relinquishing this capacity, except in their speech-making.

Upwards of 500 million people in the world are sick for lack of food. Not just some newspapers and news broadcasts, those that chronicle the degraded luxuriousness of the rich countries, but all newspapers and all news broadcasts, even those that delude themselves that they discuss important world affairs, are filled with trivia compared with this one fact. The fecundity of the human species and its success in postponing death by disease have led to a situation in which this great number of men live day in, day out, what would seem to others a living death.

Not only are there more people alive now than have ever lived in the whole of the earth's past; not only is the number doubling every generation with the inevitable unprecedented pressure on the earth's resources; the way in which we live is unprecedented and the pressures are thereby increased manifold. We demand what past generations only dreamed, that we should live continually better. There must no longer be good years and bad years but always better years, and to this end each country strives to become one great thinking organism for the advancement of whatever the technologists can discover next in the exploitation of the earth's resources. We understand nowadays, after the event, how the great growth in the mid-century in our demand for the energy to fuel the advance of industrial civilisation led us unawares into dependence on the oil-producing countries. In the same unawareness but on a vastly larger scale, we are making increasing, separate, piecemeal, potentially infinite demands on world resources and becoming ever more dependent on doing this when they are finite.

The racing pace of economic change is leading to a last and very likely in the event most explosive problem, the friction between each country's economic ambitions and those of the others. This problem is easily seen in times of world economic recession but it is a continuous fundamental problem and continuously increasing. The pattern of livelihood in each country, the movements of transition from old to new, the policies of the government for managing the development of economic prosperity are threatened by what happens in the others. If the borders of the country are open to the impact of the others, there is one kind of friction; if they are closed in an effort at insulation, there is another kind. In one form, this problem faces the industrialised countries between themselves; in another, the less developed countries between themselves; and in yet another, the industrialised and less developed countries. In each case, the time-honoured solution is the same: a struggle for mastery over what is done in other countries, a contest for power in the international economic system, beginning with some years of bargaining, advancing to pressures, deteriorating to subdued frustration and resentment, and exploding finally with force.

The view of contemporary world problems, here summarily sketched, is not just that each of them, armaments, food, natural resources and the danger of economic violence, is separately unprecedented; all share one unprecedented characteristic. In the past, each country had separate fundamental problems; the present problems face all men in all countries; they are common problems. Not just the rival possessors of nuclear arsenals but all men are in danger of death from them; the hunger of 500 million of the world's population is a world problem; the resources of nature that we depend on ever more heavily and tenuously are the earth's resources; all men face the problem of economic change and the friction and violence to which it may lead.

Just as the problems are common problems, so the right solutions require common action. If the madness of nuclear weaponry is to be checked, those countries possessed by it must guarantee the security of those that reject it and must promise that their voice shall not count for less in the affairs of the world. Common programmes of research and development will be required to enhance the ability of the starving to feed themselves and to ensure that what food is available in the world is distributed more equitably. If natural resources are to be used intelligently, economically and fairly, international authorities will be needed. Willingness on the part of poorer countries to forgo cheap but hazardous ways of producing nuclear energy will have to be matched by willingness of the richer countries to supply them with energy from the more costly, less hazardous nuclear processes that they have the means to develop. Violence arising from the friction of economic ambitions is to be avoided by willingness on the part of all countries to co-ordinate what they do economically, to make rules for the conduct of international commerce that are just, and to ensure that between the North and South of the world and within them, there is no division between rich and poor countries but a fair distribution of capacity for producing wealth.

The details of the problems and the solutions will of course change with the passing years.[1] One requirement is permanent, basic and certain: a changed public attitude to the political arrangements of the world. The problems and their solutions, whatever their changing shape in this respect or that, are beyond the capacity of 150 separate sovereign states. The old political organisation of the world corresponds no longer to the technological abilities and appetites of modern man and the consequent dangers.

'The problems posed by proliferating nuclear capabilities, poverty and hunger, environmental decay and resource depletion, population pressure and multiple infringements on human dignity, strike an increasing number of informed observers as unmanageable, given the organization of the world into about 150 sovereign states, each jealous of its own prerogatives . . . A ridiculous and tragic spectacle is that of governments who, having met to deal with the problems of poverty, population pressure, and pollution, end by celebrating the unassailability of their sovereign prerogatives . . . The crucial question is whether the statist imperatives that underlie the organization of political relations on a world scale can be re-oriented, or whether the state as such can be displaced as the central unit or organization on a world scale. The answer depends largely on the course of dominant political consciousness in the principal centers of state power. A convergent realization of common danger would greatly enhance the prospects for common solutions.'[2]

In other words, men, in keeping with the global nature of the problems facing them and the global solutions required, must adopt a global mentality. They must cease to think that their country is their only community. They must be ready to accept international imperatives and international authorities. They must accept that they are part of a community of mankind.

Let us now pause and scrutinise this view of world affairs. It has the great merit of facing facts. It is against habit, inertia and drift. Admittedly, as already mentioned, the facts presented to us continually change in detail, and some of the changes have been large. A few years ago we were warned that on present policies world population must inevitably exceed world food resources. Now it appears that the capacity of the world for increased food production is enormous and that the problem is one of maldistribution. We were similarly warned that on present methods industrial production would eventually exhaust the mineral and energy resources of the world. The latest opinion is that these resources are virtually limitless and that the problem is intelligence, economy and equity in their exploitation. The facts, in short, have changed from the quantitative, statistically demonstrable sort liked by the scientists of human affairs to the qualitative, opinionated kind that are the stock in trade of the traditional political theorist. Still, none of this counts against the spirit of the enterprise. The aim is to make us open our eyes to the world and shake us out of our conventional views. These, whatever they are, are always complacent, wishful, short-sighted and dangerous.

The question is why, despite these merits and despite the undoubted influence of this view on the climate of world opinion, it is at best only half convincing to those who make the foreign policies of states and why it cannot stand as a reformulation of the public philosophy in our time.

The trouble seems to be that it moves too easily from the facts to solutions. Between facts and solutions, there is no bridge of moral and political philosophy, no attempt to grapple with what this mankind, whose attitudes must forthwith change, is, what these states that must be summarily demoted, are. Sheer facts are relied on to arouse a sense of danger. This is without more ado dubbed a common danger, presenting common problems, requiring common solutions and belief in a community of mankind. Facts alone cannot do all this. It is doubtful, to speak theoretically, whether even the worst imaginable catastrophe facing the whole planet could be called a 'common' problem simply as a matter of fact. As things are, though all of us in the world indeed have a problem about food, we in this part of the world seem to have one problem, they in that part another; and so on as regards natural resources and the friction between national economic ambitions and even the possibility of nuclear war. Why should we in this state, they in that, think that these are 'common' problems? Why should we adopt the idea of a community of mankind? As it stands, the idea is a mere notion.

The notion seems to spring from a blend of sentimentality and intellectualism. Economists have long used the concept of 'the world economy' to describe the myriad actions, interactions and interdependencies of all men in the whole world. It is easy with a bit of enthusiasm to make an aggregate out of this, to see the world economy as a joint action by all these men, a common enterprise of a community of mankind. But why should ordinary men and statesmen think like this?

As with the common problems, so with the common solutions, sentimental aggregation takes the place of reasoning. Many of the solutions proposed for 'the predicament of mankind' involve redistribution between rich and poor, distributive justice among all men or all states. The only discernible explanation of why men and states should think in terms of distributive justice is that if one thinks for long enough about the resources of the world, one can easily slip into thinking of the world's resources, as though these really were a Gross International Product, created by the joint enterprise of the whole world and thus available for equitable distribution among the members. It is true that in national affairs some men in some countries have come to think in this collectivist way about the gross national product; but in international affairs, most do not think in this way about the resources of Argentina, Britain, Canada and the rest; and no reason is advanced why they should.

In the field of armaments and security, the proposed solutions entail various forms of undertaking by state to state. These are not of the particular sort that are often made between states that have an interest in each other's fortunes but of a generalised sort. Here our suspicion that the community of mankind is a mere notion is at its strongest; for here we have not merely our identification of a sentimental fallacy to guide us but plain experience, that of the League of Nations and United Nations. From this it seems that generalised undertakings are not the prudent way to approach the problem of conflict between states; and yet even here the proposals are made without discussion of what makes this seem so, of what men are, what states are, what the world of states is. This goodwilling, intellectualist, scientific, planetary engineering approach to world affairs ignores political experience as much as it does political philosophy. Not just as regards security guarantees but in the whole quality of its thought, starting with its impatient appeal to self-evident dangers, this view of world affairs is a resurgence of the spirit of Woodrow Wilson and the League enthusiasts of the 1920s, long since rightly castigated as mere idealism, philosophically rootless and imprudent.

A rival, much older candidate for the public philosophy for our time not only has the merit of facing facts, unclouded by idealistic notions, but comes equipped with powerful moral and political arguments. The heart of the first view was reliance on danger to make the world see reason, though no doubt some use of the idea of 'self-interest' is implied in it. The present view conversely often makes some use of the idea of danger but the heart of it is the self-interest of men and states. According to this philosophy, we must rely for the future as men always have in the past, on individual and national self-interest for defining what the problems facing us are and how they are to be tackled. No promise is made that self-interest will bring about the salvation of mankind; but it is all we have; and there are some grounds for optimism. Without having a community of mankind as its aim, self-interest, working piecemeal on problems as they arise, will very likely bring about the kinds of changes in the world's arrangements that amount to something of the sort.

The most confident expressions of this philosophy are to be found in economic affairs. The Commonwealth Secretary General, Sir Shridath Ramphal, has written:

'My proposition is that there are increasing compulsions within the global environment which make self-evident that the world is one society, a single community, and that the same interests which moved national societies to make fundamental structural adjustments now have to move the world society in the same direction. It is important to convert the North to this reality. We have to demonstrate by our actions and our conduct, why it is in the interest of the North and the South alike that the prevailing economic structures should be changed.'[3]

If in formulating a philosophy of individual and interstate affairs, the choice is between 'altruism' on the part of men and states and 'self-interest' (and according to a well-known tradition in the study of international relations, this is the choice), then certainly the right choice must be 'self-interest'. Professor Richard Cooper has mounted a shrewd attack on those who envisage a new international economic order coming about through transfers of wealth by the rich countries to the poor: the sentiment of human solidarity in the rich countries is not strong enough to bear any such conception; we should present the making of a new order, not as a zero-sum game in which the rich lose, but as a positive-sum game in which the interests of all are served.[4] Dr Vincent Cable, discussing how Britain should face the problems presented by the economic ambitions of newly industrialising countries, concluded: 'in the final analysis, the case for positive adjustment rather than protectionism rests on national economic self-interest'. He is surely right to rely on this in making the case to the British public rather than on altruism.[5]

Are these, though, the only alternatives in seeking to express the philosophy of individual and interstate relations? Though a long succession of theorists have elaborated great systems of thought according to which self-interest, decorated as one pleases, remains the foundation of politics, it is not certain that practical men and statesmen have entirely believed them or acted so. Amid the chaos and bloodshed of interstate affairs, some elements of order and peace have continuously persisted, and it is hard to believe that it is self-interest that has brought this about.

Much of international politics is, in self-interest, a zero-sum game. When the self-interest of states lies in the direction of ambition, with great powers struggling for pre-eminence in structuring international affairs and small powers seeking territory or whatever their ambition may be, what one side gains, the other must lose. When the self-interest lies in the direction of peace and quiet, what one does for its security by way of armaments and alliances diminishes the security of others. It is hard to see how anything other than continual chaos could result if self-interest were the only force at work.

In the economic sphere, it seems doubtful whether there can be an ultimate harmony of interests solely on the basis of self-interest. It is plausible perhaps that the interests of consumers in all countries are harmonious; but the interests of producers clash radically at least to the extent of the disruption of moving from a line of production in which you have been beaten to another. In the self-interested ear of governments, the sharp cries of pain from producers sound more powerfully then the diffused mutterings of consumers; and in the self-interested eyes of nations, their producers must have priority over a whole multitude of producers in foreign countries.

In recent years, states internally have become less and less free market economies fitting readily into an international market in which perhaps the prospects for an automatic harmony of interests are highest. They have become more and more tightly organised, governmentally planned and managed economic units, thus increasing the potential for conflict between them, in as much as what suits the planning and management of the one repercusses detrimentally on another. In this situation, as Professor Cooper has pointed out most vividly, states can go forward to joint international planning and management or back to national insulation, inventing new protective devices to replace the old.[6] It is not at all clear that self-interest gives any firm directive and that in so far as states do chose a more or less clear direction, it is self-interest that they are relying on for guidance.

Many have noted that self-interest is nowadays forcing states into various forms of international scientific and technical collaboration; only thus, it is said, can they afford the enormous costs. But self-interest means that the partners can only collaborate reluctantly, acrimoniously and to the minimum extent necessary to attain things that they want for their own national purposes; they cannot collaborate on things that are primarily needed by third countries, food production research, say, on behalf of the starving. The Brandt Report may have shown that North and South have much to gain in their own self-interest by co-operating; but it failed to show that it is in their self-interest to help the starving.

In the making of rules for international trade and monetary affairs it seems that pure self-interest can produce only such a struggle as to prevent any stability of rules at all. For each country must struggle for the rule which is ideal for itself; it will rarely find advantage in struggling for or even in settling for the rule which is best all round; rather than that, it will usually prefer to adhere to no rule at all or to adhere in name and then evade.

A major form of rule much discussed nowadays is 'the international regime' for the management of this or that aspect of the human environment. Once again it is hard to see how such regimes could be viable on the basis of pure self-interest. States have lately bid each other up into adopting the once ridiculed proposal that as regards the resources of the high seas each should have an exclusive 200 mile zone around its shores. Sometime in the future, just as soon as technology permits, they will very likely carve up the deep oceans as well, doubtless into selections of widespread national strips, making the map of the oceans look like a medieval three-field system. Are these arrangements the result of self-interest? We may say yes; and then accept as cheerfully as we can the kind of future that on this showing self-interest has in store for us. More likely even such dubious arrangements as these could not have been achieved by self-interest and some other factor was at work giving better grounds for hope for the future.

Many more such arguments might be brought forward, all tending to

suggest that self-interest could not be responsible for the degree of peace
and order observable in interstate affairs and that this concept cannot be
the most accurate way of expressing the public philosophy of states. But
such arguments are not the end of the matter. A profound weakness in
the self-interest view of the world, as of the benevolent view discussed
earlier, is its tendency towards intellectualism. For by 'self-interest' is
meant primarily the pursuit of interests. Yet the plain facts of history
are that states are at least as much concerned with honour, with
standing, dignity, eminence and what used to be called glory, as they
are with interests. It is as much for this reason that they desire
independence and a voice in world affairs and, if they are great powers,
supremacy. We may be tempted to call the mentality that ignores this
unwelcome fact the business mentality, the commercial view of states;
yet it was Adam Smith who wrote of individual men, 'For to what
purpose is all the toil and bustle of this world? What is the end of
avarice and ambition, of the pursuit of wealth, of power and pre-
eminence? . . . To be observed, to be attended to, to be taken notice of
with sympathy, complacency and approbation are all the advantages
which we can propose to derive from it.'[7] In dealings between states,
avowedly or not, kings have pursued this ambition and democratic
states quite as much after them, so that it has always been one of the
great forces for movement in history. There are periods when this
ambition sinks low in leading states; when that is so, nothing much
happens in world affairs, whether for good or ill. Nothing much
happens without a vision, beneficient or malign, that calls men beyond
the mere calculus of interests, and in which the reward is the self-esteem
and the esteem of others that comes from great action.

At the beginning of written political history, Herodotus put these
words into the mouth of Xerxes:

'No one need tell you of the peoples that Cyrus and Cambyses and my
father, Darius, conquered and brought into subjection, for you know
them well. Since I have sat upon this throne as my inheritance, I have
considered how I might not be outdone by those who have had that
honour before me and add no less to the Persian power. Considering
this, I find a new way for you to win new glory and a country not
smaller nor poorer than the one we inhabit but more apt than ours to
bear all manner of fruit, and in so doing requite a wrong done to you
and take vengeance. For this I have called you together, that I may lay
before you what I have in mind to do. I shall bridge the Hellespont, and
lead an army through Europe to attack Greece, so that I may exact from
the Athenians the penalty for all they have done to Persia and my
father.'[8]

Perhaps we may question the endurance of such sentiments into a time when our interest is not 'all manner of fruit' but the international economic system. Where is the glory in that? Consider, then, Professor Charles Kindleberger's analysis of the international economic system: it is not a self-equilibrating system, it always needs a stabiliser, a leader, a country willing, specifically, to maintain a relatively open market for distress goods, to provide counter-cyclical long-term lending, to provide discounting in a crisis. Britain did this till 1914; no country was able or willing to do so in the interwar years; the United States has done so since 1945 with lately flagging enthusiasm.[9] Why should any country give this leadership? There were several reasons for Britain and the United States but one plain reason was the satisfaction, both for the individual statesmen, officials and bankers concerned and for their countries as a whole, of being seen to be the one in charge, deferred to and respected.

If nothing much will be done about the problems of our time unless the leading countries are possessed by a vision of what must be done and the honour of it, the contribution that academic writers can make is restricted. They are not the ones to make the armies of Xerxes march or the American people give leadership. Still, there is one matter on which they can work. There is no honour whether for Xerxes or for the American banker unless he can claim that what he is doing is right. Indeed Professor Kindleberger's preferred word for the satisfaction that induces willingness to give leadership is not honour or prestige but 'responsibility'. States subsist at home and go into action abroad, not on the basis of altruism nor yet of self-interest, but of interest considered right. Even the philosophy of self-interest commonly admits a need to show that individual and national self-interest is right. So do the far more ferocious doctrines that from time to time scourge humanity. All seek to justify themselves as right. The sense of right has enormously reinforced the chaos and bloodshed of politics; but it is also the most likely source of the degree of order and peace that is to be found. To argue about and to suggest what is really right in opposition to hopeless, chaotic, or bloody doctrines is the task of the political theorist.

The task is not one of constructing a morality for men and states as some theorists over the centuries have apparently supposed, rationalists, utilitarians, idealists, realists, positivists, existentialists, consequentialists, and the rest; nor yet of trying to talk men into a change of heart for fear of supernatural or, nowadays, natural catastrophe. The task is to articulate the morality that men always know and to seek to draw out the implications of this in face of the new facts of a continually changing world. There are bad times for doing this when the grip of aberrant doctrines is powerful in world politics, and good times, one of which is the present. The climate of opinion in contemporary world politics, compared with the early years of this century or the 1930s, is well disposed to the idea that states in some way form a community. Statesmen engaged in international discussions or in an international conflict still indeed think in terms of 'the national interest'; but the meaning that they give to this in what they agree upon and do stretches the term beyond endurance. They use it for lack of any more acceptable articulation of the public philosophy.

The idea that there is a natural morality of men and states, a natural law, while not nowadays so unacceptable as in times past, is still surrounded by doubt. People say, 'If there is such a law, why do not all men grasp it and agree what it is?' The misunderstanding of the idea which underlies this question is the fault of many exponents of natural law of past generations. With rationalist enthusiasm, they claimed to deduce from an individualist notion of man whole detailed systems of natural laws which, of course, nobody agreed with but themselves; others, despairing of these exaggerated claims in face of the ridicule of empiricists and positivists, reduced natural law to a vague, perennial sense of right with a continually changing content. But the more readily acceptable idea of natural law is simpler than either of these. It is that just as theoretical reason in mathematics, logic and the sciences has first principles to which all reasoning must conform, so too does moral reason, and that these principles are well known to all men. This natural law is a limitation on all the countless particular judgements that we need to make about what to do and what rules to have, not a substitute for them. It is the ground in which practical wisdom, prudence, the virtue of seeing what best to do, must be rooted if it is not to be mere drifting cleverness. It does not spare us the pains of arguing, disagreeing, doing what we think right, if need be in conflict with others. It entails only that all that we argue, urge and do should be an honest effort to satisfy its principles. It entails, in other words, that moral reasoning is a search for objective truth. That is something that we all implicitly acknowledge by bothering to argue with one another.

The most basic of the principles of the natural law, the first finding of our minds when we act in the world, is that there is such a thing as good and such a thing as evil, and that good is to be done and followed and evil avoided. We find also that we are beings of a certain sort, not disposable in any direction, but having a certain inclination like the bias of a bowl, and that what furthers this inclination of our being is good and what runs counter is evil. The inclination is biological, to maintain our lives; animal, to reproduce ourselves and raise offspring; rational, to know the truth about ultimate reality, traditionally termed God, and to live in society. In that we are beings biased in these ways, we are determinate; and yet we find that we are free to override this and to live in conflict with ourselves.[10]

Each of us is a separate being in that he knows these things directly for himself, not from others, and that, in conformity with this knowledge or not, he is a separate centre of striving for a personal good.

Each of us is social, inclined to live 'in society', in that we are biased towards treating other men not as enemies, not even as indifferent but as fellow beings entitled to good treatment. We do not begin, as the individualist notion would have it, as isolated beings who then calculate that they need others and must to the extent of this need treat them well; a bias towards treating others well is the way we are. Though this is often not how we in practice feel or behave, we acknowledge it as being the true nature of man. Our being is set towards acts that respect the good of others and towards conditions that are for our good and theirs: systems for the provision of moral and material goods; customs, laws and political arrangements; prevalent social ideas. These conditions must be for the common good.

The primitive demands of the natural law are, then, that in our acts we respect parenthood, life, sexual partnership, ownership, good name. These are universally known as principles, though whether a particular act counts as an offence is sometimes a question of custom or judgement and a matter for argument between individuals and peoples. There has long been a common belief that while doubtless some such moral code as this was known from the earliest days of mankind, it was known only in relation to fellow members of the tribe, not in relation to outsiders; peaceful international relations and to this extent the alleged principles of natural law are a product of civilisation. For this belief to be substantiated, it would not be enough to show that hostility between men of different tribes was the usual state of affairs; for that might only mean that there were many justifications available which transformed the outsider into a legitimate object of attack. It would be necessary to show that in the thought-world of primitive men it was impossible ever to do wrong to an outsider in the respects mentioned. The evidence collected by Professor Numelin does not appear to support even the first of these positions, the notion of endemic hositility, leave alone the latter.[11]

We also know universally that we should assist others to avert ills or wrongs in the respects mentioned, starvation, accident, assault, and so on, and with the same difficult tasks for prudence in acting case by case. As between men of different nations, Kant wrote in *Perpetual Peace* that the only 'cosmopolitan right' was not to be treated with hostility; but perhaps he was so negative there only because he was engaged in combatting the alleged right of Europeans to subject Asians for the purposes of trade. When Perry sought to open Japan to the outside world in 1853, the Japanese negotiators, while unwilling to discuss trade as having 'no relevance to considerations of humanity', agreed to the fuelling of ships and assistance to castaways.[12] The inclination of our being to prevent ills and wrongs to others knows nothing of nation, race, religion and the like.

As to positive assistance to other men in their search for their personal good, we have an inclination towards relationships of love and friendship that involve this, reaching as far as all other men. None the less, we think that each is a separate moral being and that his own good is his responsibility, not that of others or the collectivity. Our inclination to seek the common good does not involve either dictating to others the ends they shall pursue or sacrificing our ends to those that they chose; it means only that we desire that the conditions under which all live shall be for the good of all.

When we begin to specify the conditions that make for the common good, we are no longer stating principles of natural law; we are making practical judgements. We do this, if we are prudent, in conformity with the principles and with respect for the facts of time and place, awareness at the widest of historical change.

The most basic of the conditions concerns the largest form of human political arrangement, the division of mankind into separate states, that is, separate societies under separate governments, rather than one worldwide society and one world government. About this, at least until the present period of history, there has been little controversy. For a society is an experiment in the common good and it is reasonable that there should be many of these. It would be unreasonable, moreover, that a single government, whether deliberative, executive, or judicial, should deal with such vast numbers of men in such diverse circumstances. Equally, our viciousness, overriding our inclination, requires separate states; this system is necessary to enforcing order and peace, confining collapse into chaos, providing refuge from tyranny.

So, as far as anyone can see ahead, there must be many separate states. All the time, though, their authority is limited. For the system of separate states exists for the common good. Each exists to promote the common good of its citizens. Each exists to promote in its policies towards other states the common good of its citizens and those of the other states, conditions that are for the good of all as regards systems for the provision of moral and material goods, customs, laws and political arrangements, prevalent international ideas.

The same human qualities that require a system of separate states lead to continual conflict within it and continual rejection of the pursuit of the common good. The extent of each state is not given in the nature of things; the borders of its territory or control are a matter of opinion of what is right. Each thinks that its experiment in society is superior and ought to be extended. Ample justification is thus available to the thrust of self-interest and the passion for honour. So, often, since power is distributed, is the necessary power. The enforcement of a degree of order and peace depends on self-help and, amidst ever-shifting forces, maintenance of balance.

The pressures for chaos are reinforced by plausible, even ennobling doctrines. Self-interest, we know without any telling, needs a group of collaborators; it must therefore respect morality within the group; but outside, it needs only a certain cunning circumspection. Individualist theorists elevate these commonplace facts into a doctrine, and denying a natural inclination of our being to treat other men well, proclaim the limited sovereignty of the individual and the limitless sovereignty of states: the individual agrees, because he must, to place himself under a state; and the states agree, because it is on the whole convenient, on certain customs and laws forming a states-system. In the last resort, however, all is expediency, and peace and order are at the mercy of calculation. Nationalists, transforming the idea of nature still more radically, proclaim only the historical fact of man's existence in national groups; they thereby unleash an enormous force for cohesion within the group; but since no one can know who counts as a Greek or Persian, no minority can have any security against arbitrary denunciation as a disease in the body politic; and since no one can know what is 'the Greek way' or 'the Persian way', none can resist when the most powerful and rapturous voices declare that the way is war.

Despite the frequent supremacy of these forces for chaos, the inclination to the common good has always proved stronger, pressing continuously towards order and peace. For people know that right is the norm and not an aberration; no one ever appeals to wrong to justify his actions. People know that right is not the same as self-interest or the nation; it is something to which these appeal and to which thereby self-interest clashing with self-interest, nation with nation, open themselves for judgement. People know that, in these clashes, that is right which conforms with the natural law of dealings between men and of society among men. This knowledge leaves almost everything to conflictory judgement, but not quite everything. A constant pressure is placed on the judgement of individuals and a patient force in history arises without which even power is powerless to enforce order and peace. It is this force that gives enlightenment to the self-interest of nations, inclining statesmen to more by way of respect for other nations than the theorists' doctrines can ever explain. It was this that gave some reality to the idea of a states-system among the warring states of Europe and the North, that gave some stability among the powers of the South, and that in the encounter of North and South made for some order and peace, even amidst the first ferocity, then under the empires, now in the worldwide states-system of the present. The belief, continually disregarded in the heat of ambition and power, continues unremittingly that an encounter between strangers should respect the good of each, and that in a standing relationship the conditions created should be for the good of all.

The business of foreign policy falls currently into two main areas: dealings with other states as such, and the internal affairs of other states. As to the latter, in modern European thought no theorist, it seems, has gone so far as to recommend complete indifference by the people of one state to the fortunes of people in another; but, as individualists, they have commonly conceded no more than permission to act when a state has torn up the agreement on which it is founded by tyranny or civil war; and as nationalists, they have doubted whether anyone can bring help to a nation other than the nation itself. The practice of European statesmen and peoples, on the other hand, has been much more prodigal of concern and interference.

The principle of the common good means that the internal affairs of other states are our business. For we desire as men conditions of life that are for the good of all men; a state has independence only to implement this. If the system for the production of food in a state is such that some starve; if the political arrangements are a tyranny; if in some other way, the conditions of life are not the best that can be achieved for the common good of all the people of the country, outsiders are rightly concerned and the rulers of the state are in principle accountable to them.

The application of this principle is subject to the virtue of prudence in two ways. First, the reason why the state is a separate, independent state at all is that the people and rulers are better placed to judge the requirements of the common good than we are. Second, even if we are sure that they are wrong, we may do harm by intervention or even admonition. This second point bears on the question whether it is right to criticise evils in one country while remaining silent about similar evils in another. It is wrong if it springs from connivance at these similar evils. It is right if it springs from prudence.

It may be that conditions in a country are the best that can be achieved but still some suffer great evils such as starvation. In that case, the most primitive demands of the natural law operate; we have an inclination which we should fulfil to assist other men against threats to life by lack of food or other 'basic human needs'. On the other hand, we have no obligation to any such aim as 'the economic development of developing countries' or 'closing the gap between rich and poor'. For we are not responsible for promoting the individual good of others, not even other real persons, leave alone fictitious persons, countries, states. It may be that friendship will lead us to do this; it may be that our own activities as individuals, business corporations and governments will have this result; but it is not an obligation.

Dealings between states as such create conditions under which men live in a multitude of ways. There are the systems for international trade and finance carried on by private or state corporations, and the governmental rules that regulate this. There are the international customs, laws, agreements, organisations, alliances, military relationships and defence postures. There are the ideas of what is good and evil in national and international life propagated by the leading cultures.

The basic principle of action for governments and other agents is that these conditions should be for the common good. Policy decisions on trade, finance, political and military arrangements and propaganda should have regard not only to the good of the home population but equally the good of the people of all the other states affected. Policy, whether in negotiation or conflict with other states, should indeed express 'the national interest'; for it seems that the best way for states to proceed is dialectical; but the desire behind this, the end aimed at, should be the common good.

The application of this principle to any particular matter is the job of prudence. It must reconcile the ideal and the realistic, perfect and imperfect compliance, what should best be done in the light of the facts of the matter for the common good, and what should best be done given that other parties are not seeking this at all. More with the aim of illustrating the principle than with confidence in the particular judgements that will occur, we will consider once more in conclusion the four great contemporary problems with which this chapter began.

The possession of nuclear weapons by states creates a condition of fearful risk to the life of all men. Each possessor, moreover, is threatening to do what would be wrong in terms of the most primitive demands of natural law. But the dilemma is well known. Unless all, or anyway all but one, disarm, the risk is not much diminished. Retention seems to promise that if a conventional war broke out, the scale of hostilities would be restricted by fear and no side would dare use nuclear weapons. In peacetime, no state is sole possessor of nuclear weapons so that it can bend the whole world to its will. In other words, a balance of power is maintained and this is for the good of all, large and small states alike, the righteous as much as the unrighteous.

Whether this military and political benefit outweighs the great risk is a matter of judgement; probably it does; but a corollary seems inescapable. A balance of power is never a mere negative, cancelling the power of all parties; it is a condition that enables every state to continue to exert such influence as it has; no balance, sole power, no influence. This age-old fact about a balance of power has taken on a new dimension through the invention of nuclear weapons. A nuclear balance of power means that it is only through a fearful risk to the lives of all men that states have influence. It is only because the nuclear powers risk killing everybody that they have influence. It is because nuclear powers take this risk that the lesser powers can make their voices heard. Since all benefit from the risk to all, the corollary is concern for the good of all. Nuclear weapons have in this terrifying way greatly reinforced concern for the common good in world affairs.

As regards food we have already said that where there is starvation in a country, it is the duty of other countries, by supply and research, to seek to end it. It may be that the international system for production and trade in agricultural and related products contributes to the evil; if so, the work of discovering in what ways and pressing for remedies is urgent. As regards energy and other natural resources, two views are prominent nowadays in international discussion, in some respects in tension: national sovereignty and mankind's patrimony. In both views there is some neglect of the fact that neither nations nor mankind nor even nature can take credit for the existence of natural resources; they are made by the individual men who propose to the rest of us a use for them and by the business corporations that produce them, state or private. A merely theoretical question is whether these have any obligation to put them into trade with other men; granted that they do in fact do so, their obligation is to ensure that the system of production and trade is for the common good, both within the separate state and internationally. If they fail in this obligation states may regulate them to ensure that they meet it.

As regards the tensions between the economic ambitions of states, the fundamental issue is whether autarky is permissible or whether a state is obliged to enter into the international economy. This issue is not merely theoretical. No doubt, no state at present poses the issue so starkly or considers autarky practicable. What states are often tempted to do is to plan and manage their national economies with only expedient regard for the repercussions on other states, to choose in what respects to release 'their' resources, products and capital to the outside world and to open their economies to these things from outside, and in the great dilemma for national economic policy of independence and interdependence, to think in terms wherever possible of national insulation. For such attitudes to be justifiable, there needs to be a basic principle that a state's economy is its own affair, that autarky is its fundamental right, even if not expedient.

The system of separate states, we saw earlier, does not involve a radical separateness; it exists for the common good; and we noted the social and political reasons. In economic affairs, a state must have the degree of autonomy necessary to maintaining its social and political integrity. Provided it is promoting the common good of its citizens, it is entitled to this degree of independence. In all other respects, the common good requires that states should be regions in an international economy. Their citizens should enter into international systems of commerce in resources, products, capital and technology, and should seek in doing so systems that are for the good of all. Their governments should regulate this commerce at the national borders, and make interstate rules, and plan and manage their economies not with a merely expedient but a genuine regard for the repercussions on the good of all.

To sum up: in this chapter we have reviewed three possible formulations of the public philosophy of states. Two of them, philanthropy imposed by planetary peril and national self-interest, are unrealistic. The third, the pursuit of the common good, is the natural philosophy, the norm throughout history, responsible for such peace and order as has been achieved, and continuing to work now through statesmen on the problems of our time. No one needs to be converted to the idea; all know it; at most its terms are unfamiliar. What is needed continually is to state it, to seek to fulfil it against the pressures of passion and fantastic thought, and to apply it to changing facts. There always has been a community of mankind; the problem is how to express this in action.

NOTES: CHAPTER 10

1 I have relied heavily for this statement of modern problems on the Reports of the Club of Rome.
2 Richard Falk, *A Global Approach to National Policy* (Cambridge, Mass.: Harvard University Press, 1975), pp. 3, 23.
3 'North-South dialogue', *Third World Quarterly*, January 1979.
4 'A new international economic order for mutual gain', *Foreign Policy*, Spring 1977.
5 'Britain, the "new protectionism" and trade with the newly-industrialising countries', *International Affairs*, January 1979.
6 *The Economics of Interdependence* (New York: McGraw-Hill, 1968).
7 *The Theory of Moral Sentiments*, I, iii. 2, 1.
8 Histories, VII, 8 (trans. Harry Carter, The World's Classics, London: Oxford University Press, 1962).
9 *The World in Depression 1929–39* (London: Allen Lane, 1973), ch. 14.
10 Based on Thomas Aquinas, *Summa Theologiae*, 1a 2ae, Q. 94.
11 Ragnar Numelin, *The Beginnings of Diplomacy* (London: Oxford University Press, 1950).
12 W. G. Beasley, *Select Documents on Japanese Foreign Policy 1853–68* (London: Oxford University Press, 1955), p. 126.

11
An Ethic of Responsibility

MOORHEAD WRIGHT

'The objective of responsible men everywhere, today, is that of building "a world at peace"'.[1] What is one to make of such a sweeping pronouncement? It seems to impose an obligation on all men, regardless of any special roles they may have (for example, statesman or diplomat), to undertake the task of bringing about world peace. But how could the average citizen be expected to carry such a burden? Does he have a duty to do so even if he has in the ordinary course of his life little opportunity or occasion to improve the prospects for world peace? Or does 'responsible' here simply mean good or virtuous, and is 'peace' held to be the sort of objective which such a good or virtuous man would naturally seek?

These are the sorts of questions which are often raised in talking about international politics, where responsibility is frequently at issue. In any situation of conflict or co-operation, the actors involved may endeavour to establish claims about responsibility. They may attempt to take, reject, shift, impose, deny, or share responsibility. Similarly, any individual or collectivity may be said to be responsible or irresponsible, or we may try to 'hold it responsible' for some action or omission.

The most general covering notions for the kinds of statements in which we use the concept of responsibility are ascriptions, attributions and imputations; the last is usually reserved for negative, fault-finding usages. The meaning of the concept itself varies with the context, whether legal, moral, or political, and many interesting problems arise from the interaction of these contexts.

In this chapter I intend to examine the main grounds for the attribution of responsibility in international politics, isolate three core meanings of responsibility and relate them to traditional concepts of political theory, and finally assess the prospects for a normative theory of responsibility in international politics.

THE GROUNDS FOR ATTRIBUTIONS OF
RESPONSIBILITY

The language of both practitioners and scholars reveals a variety of grounds for the attribution of responsibility in international politics. For example, in his Notre Dame speech of 22 May 1977, President Carter called on the Soviet Union 'to join with us and other nations in playing a larger role in aiding the developing world'. The Soviet Union, he implied, had an 'obligation' to embark upon 'common aid efforts' with the United States.[2] This appeal was likely to fall upon deaf ears, however, since the Soviets accept no responsibility for the problems of the developing world; in fact they claim that Western colonialism is to blame. Here we have two different kinds of attribution of responsibility, one positive, the other negative. The Soviet view, furthermore, would hold that those who are said to be responsible in the negative sense (that is, those who they allege impoverished the Third World by colonial exploitation) should take responsibility in the positive sense (that is, by giving foreign aid). The link here is basically the notion of reparation, or restitution, namely, that one should undo or pay compensation for the harm or injury which one has done to others in the past. This is rightfully a key notion in legal theory, but in political contexts it is more dubious. In the above case, for example, it is often denied that Western colonialism was responsible (in a causal sense) for Third World poverty.

Another strategy is to ground responsibility on a collective good such as peace. Such an appeal underlies another passage from President Carter's Notre Dame speech: 'We know a peaceful world cannot long exist one-third rich and two-thirds hungry.'[3] Peace is here said to be the common value shared by the North and the South which justifies the North 'taking' responsibility for alleviating poverty and hunger in the South. Although this form of attribution does not suffer the handicap of the reparation view of responsibility, it is questionable whether a collective good such as peace offers a strong enough motivation for such disparate groups of states as make up the international system.

A third alternative is to attribute responsibility to a transcendental value, for example, reason or charity, or to a transcendental being. Writing in *The Times* (2 September 1978), the theologian R. P. C. Hanson comments:

'Christians, and not only Christians but all monotheists, Jews, Muslims and Sikhs as well, believe that we are responsible to God for our actions and that God will not allow us to shift that responsibility on to others. God is judging and punishing each of us according to our deserts.'

This idea of responsibility to God also lies behind the concept of 'stewardship' which theologians employ to justify man's responsibility for conserving and sharing scarce natural resources and protecting the global environment. In other words, man is seen as God's 'steward' or 'deputy' on earth, responsible for 'distant' as well as 'near neighbours'.

Another ground for responsibility may be a specific formal commitment such as an international agreement, charter, or treaty. As an example here is a passage from President Carter's United Nations speech of 17 March 1977:

'All the signatories of the United Nations Charter have pledged themselves to observe and to respect basic human rights. Thus, no member of the United Nations can claim that mistreatment of its citizens is solely its own business. Equally, no member can avoid its responsibilities to review and to speak when torture or unwarranted deprivation occurs in any part of the world.'[4]

In this case responsibilities are held to be based upon adherence to an international convention and upon membership in the formal organisation which it established. It does not of course follow that all members would agree with President Carter's interpretation of these responsibilities; if the UN's past record on human rights is any guide, most in fact would not. The varying interpretations do however highlight the discretionary element which is an intrinsic part of the notion of responsibility in most social and political contexts; in contrast strict legal or moral duties allow no room for discretion.

Yet another basis for the attribution of responsibility is power, and not surprisingly this figures prominently in international politics. Take for instance George Liska on *Imperial America*: 'an empire or imperial state is . . . a state that combines the characteristics of a great power, which being a world power and a globally paramount state, becomes automatically a power primarily responsible for shaping and maintaining a necessary modicum of world order'.[5] The automatic nature of this process is somewhat suspect, but the assumption behind it is that great power necessarily casts a nation into a leadership role with its attendant burdens. After Vietnam Richard Rosecrance sees the reverse process at work:

'Once so dominant in the international arena, America has become an ordinary country in foreign relations . . . she cannot be expected to take on special responsibilities for world peacekeeping, to use her military forces where others do not wish to become involved, to support the world economy and sustain an international financial structure organized around the dollar.'[6]

We shall return to power later in the chapter, but here we note the close correlation between power and responsibility in discussions of international politics.

A closely related ground for the attribution of responsibility is one's role or position in a social or political institution or relationship. For example, familial responsibilities are analysed in terms of the roles of husband and wife or parents and children. Legal responsibility is located in the relationships between certain kinds of parties or 'legal persons', for example, the vendor and purchaser in a contract of sale. 'Responsible government' is examined by political theorists in terms of a relationship between the rulers and the ruled. What these relationships have in common is that they subsist between roles (rather than individuals) and are often constituted and regulated by rules, whether formal or informal. There are similar role structures in international politics, for example, belligerent and neutral in war, alliance partners, donor and recipient country in foreign aid programmes, importer and exporter in foreign trade, guardian and ward in colonial relationships, patron and client state in hegemonial relationships.

THE MEANINGS OF RESPONSIBILITY

Our survey of the most common grounds for the attribution of responsibility in international politics has revealed a mixture of descriptive and evaluative, positive and negative, and retrospective and prospective usages of the concept. But, as many of our examples suggest, the concept is most often used in the rhetoric of advocacy; hence we need to probe deeper into the conceptual and normative bases of the idea if we are to construct a genuine ethic of responsibility in international politics.

The enterprise may seem beset with difficulties due to the wide variety of senses in which the word is used, but there are three core meanings on which to build a theory of moral responsibility. These are:

(1) accountability or liability for choices, decisions and exercises of judgement in the light of relevant rules or laws;
(2) the rational and moral exercise of discretionary power in the light of a sound calculation of probable consequences and a fair evaluation of claims;
(3) responsiveness to the needs or claims of others.[7]

It is apparent that these are not completely separate meanings but rather related facets of a single meaning.

Accountability and responsibility share the same root – making a response, answering, or giving an account – to which the element of 'requiredness' is added. The etymology of responsibility gives an interesting clue to the origins of this requiredness: the Latin verb *spondeo*, the root of 'respond' and its cognates, means to promise solemnly; to bind, engage, pledge oneself (verbal contracts in civil law); promise for another, become his security; promise sacredly, give assurance; promise, pledge on behalf of a government. The verb *respondeo* means to promise or offer in return, to answer, to repay or return. These meanings all convey the idea of a voluntary commitment or self-imposed constraint which becomes the basis of duty or obligation. 'Requiredness' is thus an integral part of the idea of responsibility.

Although the original contractual overtones may not have survived, we are clearly dealing in cases of responsibility with some form of constraint, whether internal or external, whether *to* someone or *for* something or both. Furthermore, the notion of 'giving an account' entails the reasoned justification of one's conduct or actions or character, and to be successful it must be persuasive, that is, command the assent of those to whom it is addressed. Hence the second and related core meaning, which emphasises deliberation and rationality. This sense of the word also covers the capacity or disposition for such exercise of discretionary power.

The phrase 'discretionary power' indicates the close links which responsibility has with the concepts of freedom and power. Discretion means the freedom to choose, so that responsibility can only be attributed to an autonomous individual, or, more arguably, to an independent collectivity such as a government, cabinet, or nation-state. Autonomy or freedom in this context means at least the absence of external compulsion, but it also means 'the power or capacity of judging the relative value or worth, the rightness or wrongness of the alternative acts and their probable consequences and of acting accordingly'.[8] Now it is clear that power or capacity in this latter sense is not something which in most cases is either absolutely present or absolutely absent, but is present in varying degrees. This gives rise to serious controversies about the extent to which a given action is determined or freely chosen, especially with regard to liability for punishment, and the grounds for resolving such controversies are the subject of much philosophical literature. The main point to be made here is that as there are degrees of freedom, so there are degrees of responsibility. The concept of a responsible moral agent does however entail a minimum capacity for rational deliberation.

Freedom means power *to* make moral and rational decisions, but these decisions often involve power *over* others, hence limiting their freedom and posing some of the classical dilemmas of political theory. It follows that, to the extent that we restrict the freedom of others, contributing thereby to the causation of their conduct or action, we must assume proportionate responsibility for their conduct or action. Thus power and responsibility are logically connected as well. In most actual political activities there is of course a constant tendency to separate them, that is, to exercise 'power without responsibility'. Such political arrangements as constitutions and charters are deliberate attempts to join in fact two ideas which are joined in logic, that is, to guarantee the 'responsibility of power' within a given public domain.

In addition to freedom and power, there is another concept to be added to our cluster of related ideas – community. It is here that the third core meaning of responsibility – responsiveness to the needs and claims of others – becomes dominant, for we assume that communal bonds of some kind link us with those for whom we feel responsible in this sense. Such communities may be based on close, face-to-face relationships, for example, family, neighbours, or friends, or they may comprise more abstract, large-scale relationships, such as nation, culture, religion, or even 'humanity'. There are various ways in which these relationships can be envisaged. One model is a series of expanding, concentric zones, representing either such specific types of reference group as those mentioned above or what Harold Lasswell describes as 'zones of interaction' – identity, organisation, action, opinion and attention.[9] Another approach is to extend metaphorically a term used for a proximate relationship to a more extended one, for example, the concept of 'distant neighbour' in Christian ethics.

Inherent in each of the three ideas we have been discussing (power, freedom and community) is the element of limit or boundaries. It is important to stress this aspect of the theory of responsibility which we are advocating. Ascriptions of responsibility cut two ways: they may enlarge the range of actions which we are enjoined to do or to forbear from doing, but they restrict it at the same time. In other words, it follows from this theory that everyone is not responsible for everything or to everyone. As one writer observes in discussing world hunger: 'It is morally debilitating to accept more responsibility than we can bear.'[10] Psychologically, too, shifts of responsibility can be unsettling, both for individuals and nations. Taking away responsibility lessens one's burden but casts doubt upon one's ability or competence; adding responsibility calls for extra effort or perhaps an adjustment to a new identity.

AN ETHIC OF RESPONSIBILITY

Max Weber first put into general circulation the idea of an 'ethic of responsibility', which he contrasted with an ethic of absolute or ultimate ends.[11] Raymond Aron and, most recently, Stanley Hoffmann have advocated such an ethic, but neither has given it much elaboration beyond calling attention to the central importance of consequences in ethics.[12]

Our previous survey of the three core meanings of responsibility gives us the basis for developing such an ethic by providing three criteria for responsible statesmanship. In the first place, accountability stresses the 'to' aspect of responsibility. Statesmen are accountable to their own citizens, it is true, but also to their peers in the states system. In a general way such accountability is a product of the general rules and laws of the states system, however few and weak these may be in comparison to domestic ones in certain types of democratic polities. In a more restricted sense, a statesman is accountable to those counterparts with whom he has more immediate and closer ties. For example, a NATO statesman is accountable to his alliance partners, a responsibility which is partly engineered into the formal consultative arrangements of the alliance but which is also a product of informal relationships of individual statesmen and ministers. A similar phenomen may be emerging from the annual economic summits of the heads of state of the major industrial nations, which over time take on some of the qualities of an 'institution'.

It should be stressed that accountability does not necessarily mean that 'good conduct' will be ensured, but it does call for some explanation or justification of one's conduct. That reasons for one's actions or policies are expected by those whom they affect significantly is an irreducible minimum for an international morality.

The second criterion – rational and moral deliberation – is connected with the first, for giving reasons is an important aspect of rationality. Such deliberation is the burden which freedom places on an individual: if he is free to decide, he ought to decide well. An important feature of rational deliberation is the sound calculation of consequences, within the limitations of human foresight and the play of chance. Political morality, it is often argued, is primarily consequentialist in the absence of a fundamental moral consensus. No less frequently however have critics of utilitarianism decried this emphasis on consequences. Short of a revival of natural law ethics, for which Michael Donelan argues eloquently in the previous chapter, consequences are likely to hold sway.

This criterion not only urges us to attend to the consequences of our actions but also calls for 'a fair evaluation of claims', that is, justice. This bears on the third criterion, a responsiveness to the needs and claims of others. It must be conceded that this criterion has the least secure footing in international politics, which has traditionally been the domain of exclusive loyalties and limited sympathies. The concentric-circles model discussed earlier remains the prevailing view, but as Henry Shue has argued recently, there are no good *moral* reasons why responsibility should weaken as we move outwards from the centre.[13]

An important distinction here is between special and general obligations. We have special obligations to our family, colleagues, compatriots, but we have general obligations to all those whose welfare is likely to be affected by our actions or omissions. It is often argued that in cases of conflict special obligations take precedence over general ones, but it is by no means clear from a moral standpoint why this should be so. Once we admit the desirability of 'responsiveness to the needs and claims of others', then we are bound to make the urgency and seriousness of these needs as much a consideration as any shared characteristics or affinities. This does not mean that we have unlimited responsibilities, for as we have argued earlier the idea of limits or boundaries is intrinsic to an ethic of responsibility. The question which has to be answered is where to draw the boundaries and how to justify the decision.

Summing up, we can say that an ethic of responsibility enjoins us to account for our actions, decide rationally and respond to the needs of others. The main point of this chapter has been to show that these imperatives, though not widely followed in the present international system, are not unrealistic or utopian. They do not imply a view of human nature as either perfectible or inherently evil. Nor do they leave us with only the despairing counsels of the so-called realists for whom the only scope for moral choice lies in opting for the 'lesser of two evils'. Its central notion, moreover, is one which is already part of the everyday ethical, legal and political discourse of international politics.

NOTES: CHAPTER 11

1 L. J. Halle, '"A World at Peace"', *Encounter*, vol. 36, no. 2 (1971), p. 48.
2 President Carter, 'A foreign policy based on America's essential character', *Department of State Bulletin*, vol. 76 (1977), p. 624.
3 ibid.
4 President Carter, 'Peace, arms control, world economic progress, human rights: basic priorities of U.S. foreign policy', *Department of State Bulletin*, vol. 76 (1977), p. 332.
5 G. Liska, *Imperial America: The International Politics of Primacy* (Baltimore, Md: Johns Hopkins University Press, 1967), p. 10.
6 R. Rosecrance (ed.), *America as an Ordinary Country: U.S. Foreign Policy and the Future* (Ithaca, NY: Cornell University Press, 1972), p. 11.
7 The first two meanings are found in J. R. Pennock, 'The problem of responsibility', in C. J. Friedrich (ed.), *Responsibility* (New York: Liberal Arts Press, 1960), pp. 9, 13. The third is based on J. Fletcher, *Moral Responsibility: Applications of Situation Ethics* (Philadelphia, Pa: Westminster Press, 1967), ch. 14.
8 M. Ginsberg, *On Justice in Society* (London: Heinemann, 1965), p. 169.
9 H. D. Lasswell, 'Future systems of identity in the world community', in C. E. Black and R. A. Falk (eds), *The Future of the International Legal Order*, Vol. IV, (Princeton, NJ: Princeton University Press, 1972), pp. 11–13.
10 L. B. Smedes, 'Hunger and Christian duty', *Worldview*, vol. 19, no. 5 (1976), p. 40.
11 M. Weber, 'Politics as a vocation', in *From Max Weber: Essays in Sociology* (London: Kegan Paul, Trench Trubner, 1947), pp. 126–7.
12 R. Aron, *Peace and War* (Garden City, NY: Doubleday, 1966), pp. 629–35; S.

Hoffmann, *Duties beyond Borders: On the Limits and Possibilities of Ethical International Politics* (Syracuse, NY: Syracuse University Press, 1981), pp. 12, 28–9.

13 H. Shue, *Basic Rights: Subsistence, Affluence, and U.S. Foreign Policy* (Princeton, NJ: Princeton University Press, 1980), ch. 6.

12
Language, Culture and the Concept of International Political Community

ALAN PLEYDELL

In this chapter I wish to raise the question whether there are not, after all, really serious obstacles to our all living together in a single community of moral obligation as for instance our Christian and liberal or Kantian traditions seem to require of us, because of their emphasis on universal duties, and whether none the less there might hot still be some way of moving in the direction of these requirements without simply ignoring the obstacles or pretending they are not there.

The perspective of the chapter is somewhat different from most of the others in this book and the argument is likely to appear strange to the reader. This is basically on account of two reasons. First, the body of reflection on which it is built is a long way removed from the standard literature on international relations and its conceptual vocabulary, so that its terms may be unfamiliar to most students of the subject.[1] Secondly, the problem it deals with is not immediately recognisable as a problem of international relations at all because it is not, on the face of it, concerned with those tangible features of the contemporary international world with which we are all familiar, such as states, international organisations, military alliances, and so forth, so much as the much more nebulous notions of language and cultural identity. Nevertheless, the problem I shall discuss, namely, the *prima facie* incompatibility between a plural world of deep-seated cultural identities and the possibility of a single world community of values,[2] underlies in a fundamental way not only the contemporary international predicament but also the predicament of men living together on the same planet with one another at any time. Nor, as I shall try to show, can this predicament be sidestepped by alluding to the contemporary phenomenon of the erosion of cultural differences, for this erosion in itself represents a movement not towards moral or political community so much as a common alienation from the only condition in which in principle we could be in a communitarian relation with one another, namely, one in which our separate rootedness, identity and self-possession were acknowledged.

Basically, I think, we have made the problem of thinking about international community too easy for ourselves by assuming that community consists in being *like* one another in various respects, so that for instance we should have more of a community if we all agreed to share common 'goals', or if we were united by a common legal system, or by a common ideology, or by a common culture, or by a common economic system. As a matter of fact I think that in all these respects we are indeed coming to resemble one another more and more and with ever greater rapidity, simply as a consequence of the material interpenetration of one another's lives, and this is what we mean by cultural integration. But this integration is not at all the same thing as belonging to a world community. Nor does it produce anything which we should grace by the name of world culture. Cultural integration is in fact nothing more than cultural dissolution unless it carries with it the development of new specific collective identities in different parts of the world which perpetuate the phenomena of human difference and difference of outlook, and creativity.

I shall begin by showing how common culture on the one hand and political community on the other are generated by different aspects or modes of the same defining criterion of humanity, namely language, dealing with each in turn. I shall pass on to the consideration of how it is that a political community can arise out of a certain kind of culture and 'civilise' it. Whereas cultures which have not arrived at the stage of political community are likely to find it very difficult to get on with one another, those which are 'civilised' by the development of a self-conscious public realm ought to find the development of relations with one another both relatively easy and mutually advantageous. It is this latter situation which I shall refer to as international community. Thus I shall show that there is an internal relation between the quality of a constitution at home, that is to say its being a public realm in the full sense, and the possibility of enjoying communitarian relations abroad. I shall conclude with a discussion of whether membership of such a community, which is of course an idealisation, although I hope a useful one, rather than a description of the world as it is, would necessarily entail common rules and if so of what kind.

I

Language is part and parcel of what makes us human in a central way.

Because we have it we also have a notion of what we are, what we do and what the world is like. The words we use characterise our situation, and in the absence of language we should not have any idea of it but simply be an indistinguishable part of the overall state of affairs. In any language there is an overall story or structured picture in which each of the elements of life and the constituents of the world has its place. Language is not merely a window on the world; rather, the structure of the particular language which we speak stamps its own impression on the world as we understand it. It gives the world a particular character or flavour as well as recording it. If we spoke in another way, for instance as the Hopi Indians do, then the world as a whole would seem very different to us. The verb structure of their language led the man who first studied it to conclude that they understand time and space in quite different ways than we do, so that in a real sense we inhabit quite different imaginational worlds.[3]

There is not just one language, there are many. Language is not in the first place generated by individuals but by groups.[4] And different languages are brought into being by different groups which live in different places at different times. The languages are different in the first place because the overall experiences of the different groups are different. But the difference is much more radical than this because it is in principle possible that *any* language which more or less worked for the purpose of communication *could* arise in the environmental situation of just one group. So in a sense the actual language which happens to arise in a particular place at a particular time is arbitrary, although that is not the way it seems from within the perspective of the language itself.

This self-understanding imparted to a group by its language we can call a cultural identity, or simply a culture. It is the same thing as what anthropologists mean by a culture – that integral series of practices and their explanation which form the life of the group as a whole and which locate it in the world and make it a significant part of the order of things as a whole.

If this account is more or less right then the central fact about humanity is that it is naturally divided in the first place into a series of *essentially* different collectively held perspectives on the nature of the world, the nature of man and the point of human existence. The lives of these groups, we shall say, are essentially communal in that the members of each group live an integrated and organic life together. The life of the individual is merged in that of the group and gains its significance as a part of the whole.

Given this state of affairs, if cultures have little experience of one another and their different circumstances of life, it is highly likely that there will be little or no felt distinction between life as lived by the group and life as such. That which is closest to home and is most familiar appears most natural. In fact what is close is so familiar and so unquestionable, since it contains our sense of reality, that it is scarcely noticed. Our own language, and the practices and understandings which are bound up in it, are not curious objects of attention for us but like a second skin. Each culture, therefore, looks from the inside not self-consciously like the life of *our* group, *our* way of life, but just life.

If cultures approximate to this type on the whole, and there is some historical evidence that they do so,[5] at least in the early stages of human development, we can also see that there will be a natural state of war between them if they happen to come into too close a proximity, and then the weakest will simply succumb. This naturally warlike character of human cultures, that they bristle with hostility on the outside, is simply the outward aspect of a collective mentality which is inwardly solipsistic. What makes it possible to obliterate outsiders is that they simply don't come into the picture, and even when they do obtrude themselves inescapably they are likely to appear extremely strange and not at all the sort of people, if people at all, with whom it is possible to treat seriously. If this account seems excessively bizarre or irrelevant, we need only remember that it is less than a hundred years ago that precisely this fate overran the indigenous population of North America.

All this is attributable to what I call the 'substantive' aspect of language. We occupy this aspect of our language when we are so to speak just cruising along in it in neutral. Then its principal function is to transmit to us the attitudes and understandings which are already embedded in its structure and vocabulary as a result of the cumulative consolidation of past usage. That is, we do not use our language deliberately and actively in the conscious expression of new thoughts, or to bring about new understandings of the whole order of things, so much as to re-enact past actions and significances in the present, and thus provide ourselves with historical continuity, memory, and an ordered world of sense, belonging and the given intelligibility of things. The substantive aspect of our language is that which particularises, roots and grounds us. There is never any moment, when we are speaking at least, when this aspect is not present – because the majority of words and grammatical structures that we use, even if we are innovating, are necessarily the product of the past. But of course there is variation in the extent to which this substantive aspect is predominant. When it has the upper hand, then our collective past, our inherited and particular identity and understanding articulates itself through us and thus reinaugurates itself – our lives are lived according to habit. When it is relatively in abeyance then there is room for a restructuring of our world of understanding to meet new and apparently incompatible circumstances. This is what happens when we are actively thinking and is what active thought, as opposed to general awareness, consists in. It is attributable to the other aspect of language use, its 'formal' mode.

I shall return to the implication of the formal mode for the development of political community shortly. Let me, first, however, point to a problem which arises from our necessary reliance on the substantive aspect of language. When this aspect is excessively predominant, for example when our reactions to events are bound by ritual, we are driven into making a kind of systematic mistake about the character of the world, though one which it is natural to make. This mistake consists in assuming from the correct premise that the perspective afforded by our language is necessary, for we always need *some* perspective as a starting-point, the false conclusion that our *particular* perspective is necessary and is coincident with the world, so that there is nothing more to learn. We think that our mode of understanding is adequate and final, when of course in reality it never is. This is what effectively happens when a collective culture identifies itself and its vision with reality.

I said above that there is a natural tendency for cultures to gravitate towards this mistake of collective solipsism. This is because of two facts about cultures in their natural state. The first is relative inexperience of other cultures and therefore unawareness that there are other perspectives on reality afforded by other languages; the second is living an undifferentiated life within the culture. Communal language, in order to function effectively, *has* to be comparatively repetitive and to represent a more or less unitary perspective. Otherwise easy communication would break down, and more importantly, so would the sense of natural affinity and harmony which comes from not having constantly to question what everybody else means. There is therefore great comfort in not saying new things, or saying things in radically new ways, but in repeating the old. And it is socially cohesive.

However, the cost of an exclusively communal life is precisely that it stultifies the development within the group of different perspectives, and without these there cannot be new thought and enlarged understanding of the world as it actually is. So the life of collective cultures is internally relatively comfortable and reassuring whilst at the same time being externally precarious. And the precariousness of the situation is brought about by the mentality of the collective group in association with, that is to say in opposition to, the corresponding mentalities of the other collective groups.

II

In contrast to the tendency towards cultural solipsism which arises from excessive dependence on the always necessary, identity-forming, substantive aspect of our language, it is the formal aspect which may generate political community within a culture, and civilise it. It essentially consists in being related to language and experience with a different attitude of mind.

In turning to this second aspect of language I should first explain what I mean by the notion of community. Community is the coming together of different people with different perspectives and ideas of the nature of the world, each in the truthful recognition of the inadequacy of his own perspective as an understanding of the world and of the need to complement his perspective with that of others despite and because of their manifest difference and seeming incompatibility. The partners in a community do not seek to blend or merge their differences, because their differences are all that each uniquely has to give and because they understand that it is the creative tension between the differences which leads to a growth in each of knowledge and understanding of the real world. Thus each is not reduced but fulfilled in the production of something new. The mentality which accompanies the move towards community is not an inherited experience of natural affinity with others but the felt recognition of difference, and a knowledge of one's own ignorance and partiality. Whereas our culture is a residue of the past both necessary to our vitality and orientation in the world and never entirely relinquished, the singular source of the perspective which we bring to our relationship with others, community is always something in the making which is never entirely achieved. It is an essentially mobile relationship in which the members understand consciously that they are changed and refreshed by their mutual influence, whilst remaining distinct. The central point to recognise is that community both implies and requires the continuation of substantive differences between the persons who make it up in order to continue in growth. A merging and mutual dissolution of substantive identities between persons, therefore, such as was portrayed in my description of a collective culture, is the very antithesis of community. And by extension, a merging and dissolution between different collective cultures would be taking away from us even what we have, a given partial identity and place in the world.

The formal, as distinct from substantive, aspect of language comes to the fore when we *use* language to express new understandings which approximate more comprehensively than our old habitual language to the world as we find it. New thoughts do not emerge out of the continuous stream of repetitive collective talk – this is merely the reiteration of past thoughts which are now part of the unreflective general background of assumptions and which are therefore thoughts no longer, but mere familiar aspects of the imagination which, when simply assumed and inhabited as second nature, actually block off our access to new thought and continuing awareness. Real thought begins when the stream of collective talk ceases. It is then that the individual, and only individuals are capable of thinking, falls into reflection. Only in silence can a reorientation of the attention away from the cloying attachment of the inherited overall structure of significances take place.

The beginning of thought is the recognition of a tension or incompatibility in the things that are present to our mind – those things that are taken up by our wandering imaginations, fragments of past talk and present experience. We have successfully had a new thought when we have not simply imagined the incompatible things in themselves, but conceived the form of the relationship between them which makes them part of the same integral and broader reality yet without dissolving them. We have spoken a new thought when we have encapsulated this relationship in language. The expression of thoughts is the reordering of old words in absolutely new senses, so that relationships not previously present to mind, let alone understood, are now seen in a more proper light, that is, more justly. When each of us thinks, he generates a plurality of opposed objects of attention in his mind which are then reintegrated, if he is successful, in a broader, more tightly disciplined and satisfactory pattern. And when he speaks, if he is speaking a new thought, he makes this reorientation of understanding available to others. Thus thought is transmitted from one to another, but only if the recipient is capable of thinking the same thought by himself, that is, conceiving, it may be out of different material, the same formal and objective relationship.

Note that there is a homologous pattern, an identity, between what – on the view offered here – happens in our minds when we are thinking and what happens to the group when it is transformed from a culture with a single overall perspective and account of life into a community founded on a multiplicity of perspectives. There is a change from imaginational stasis to creation. If a man is to think, then there must be a free play in the elements of his imagination so that new antithetical tensions can arise in his mind which are then resolved by incorporation into broader pictures. The precondition of this process is that he be fished out of the general stream of reiterative collective language and imagination – and this is exactly what happens if he has the opportunity to fall into thought. At the same time, the precondition of a creative community arising out of a homogeneous group culture is that its members be able to become different in their imaginations so that they may then come together again creatively in the exchange of differently grounded ideas which are food for further thought on the nature of the community as a whole. There must therefore be within the culture, if it is to be transformed into a community, a realm within which it is possible to be away from the influence of the collective mind. It is only then that imaginational difference can arise to some degree amongst its members.

In other words, a static collective culture becomes a political community if and only if there develops within it a sufficient enclave of privacy for at least some persons to stand apart from the group and one another and work things out for themselves. Only on this basis can they become different in their imaginations and only on this basis can they rejoin one another creatively in a group which collectively and self-consciously begins to understand its own evolving situation and to move away from random evolution and towards conscious self-direction. Such a group would be able to take stock of its own milieu, and decide what to do, case by case, on the basis of reason, moral, prudential and every other form, in its relations with the outside world.

This process of separation and reintegration is the precondition for the creation of a public realm, a *res publica*. It sounds like a contradiction in terms, since I have argued that only individuals can think, but really there is no paradox. In a static communal culture there is no distinction between public and private realms. As a consequence there is no significant imaginational variation between its members, hence its life is repetitive and comparatively unvarying, and its members, being immersed in the general stream of univocal talk, have not the wherewithal to think. Therefore, neither the members considered singly, nor the group considered as a whole, think or understand in any creative way or adapt other than traditionally and emotionally to new circumstances. Conversely, in a political community the citizens have different imaginations and are therefore at least able to think. Being able to think they are able to conceive, from the standpoint of their quite different perspectives, the same formal thought, which perhaps is expressed in different ways, that there is a rational profit both to each and to all in coalescing in a public realm for the mutual exchange of ideas concerning the lives of each and all. This exchange includes deliberation on the question of where and how the dividing line between public and private should fall, and the character of foreign relations, both in general and in particular. They are also capable of deciding together what shall constitute a decision between them which will bind them in future; they are able to generate formal rules or procedural laws about deciding to decide. A public body can make their collective acts rational, and therefore thoughtful, by deeming that certain procedures shall be considered to constitute public acts.

What we have described is the transformation by thought of a univocal, static culture into a creative plural and public community. Imagination, which was a collectively unfolding thing, most obviously expressed in myth, is now the private property of the individual. In this sense the culture, the collective unthinking mentality of communal imagination has been destroyed and fragmented into individual and different creative imaginations. The solidarity and feeling of absolute preference for the group, the sense of sameness, which was also the basis for a natural and unthinking indifference or hostility to all other groups has now been destroyed, because that very solidarity and feeling of preference for the native group was founded on collective imagination. Solidarity now has a quite different basis. It is not just huddling together for security against the demons which lurk without, that mentality induced by what I have called collective solipsism. On the contrary, the solidarity of the new public community is based on plurality, on the citizens all having different imaginations, and the common recognition of the fruitfulness of plurality.

The most important point to notice about this civilisation of culture is that it has removed the one obstacle to understanding and responding rationally and morally to those who previously lay outside the orbit of the collective imagination of the group, and therefore did not, even potentially, come within the scope of its moral attention. That obstacle was the stultified collective imagination itself. We started with a natural and irreducible war between a plurality of collective solipsisms. If we generalise the argument from one *res publica* to many, we wind up with a world constituted by a plurality of public realms whose ways of life are guided by reason, including of course moral reason. Whereas in the world of solipsistic cultures there was an absolute barrier, on all sides, to an understanding of what lay beyond the particular culture, in a world of political communities all are potentially open to rational and thoughtful accommodation to one another.

The introduction of reason into cultures so that they become creative and civilised republics transforms the psychological function of sameness and difference in the world. In the world of warring cultures there were no really differentiable intelligent human individuals, there was above all the collective group mentality, which was not itself very intelligent and was swayed by feeling and imagination, but which served adequately so long as each culture remained by itself. The main difference was not between persons but between cultures, and it made relations with the outside world for each culture essentially both arbitrary and bloody because of their mutual incomprehensibility. Sameness was solidarity and comforting; difference bred trouble. But when reason mediates the imagination and creates plural communities, substantive difference between imaginations is imported within the former psychological boundary of the group and now stands between human individuals instead of between collective cultures. That is the change in its structure. But as well as changing place, imaginational difference is not now the source of hostility between individuals but the basis of community between them.

It is because difference in imagination has changed its function from being a cause of hostility to a reason for solidarity that there is now no residual obstacle to considering peoples who formerly lay outside the pale of the collective culture by reason of difference in imagination, as potentially party to the public realm. The fact that other people are different now no longer causes the group to be indifferent or hostile to them. But it does create a motive for seeking relationship with them, simply because difference is understood to provide the basis of fruitful exchange and because difference in itself, if we reflect on it, reminds us of our partiality, the lack of completeness of our lives and of our understanding. Once we understand that we are ignorant we also understand that there is profit and potential development in the juxta-position of opposites in human language, imagination and understanding.

III

We have arrived at a world of pluralistic and open republics from the starting-point of a world of monolithic and closed collective cultures. We have moved from a sort of basic primeval irrationalism to a world of perfect and creative co-operation and harmony between men by so to speak turning the key of reason in the lock of language. In so doing we have shifted identity from being a communal possession of the group to a private possession of the individual and so removed what I take to be the central obstacle to a practical moral solidarity between human beings as a whole, namely, our habit of attaching ourselves in our imagination and hence in our moral commitments to groups which are always more than the individual but always less than mankind as a whole. Of course this idealised sketch of what is involved has only been achieved on paper but it is worth asking none the less what conclusions flow from it.

The first and most obvious conclusion is that although we started from a very different set of original conditions, at least it certainly looks that way on the surface, we have wound up with a solution which is to all intents and purposes exactly the same as the conclusion arrived at by Kant – enlightened solidarity between men is both brought into being and served by a plural world of republican constitutions. This leads on to the thought that it may be possible to converge on this same conclusion, that peace is served by republican constitutions, and that peace is simply another name for international community, from a number of different starting-points.

The particular route by which I have arrived at this conclusion, however, has an important specific bearing on how we can conceive of an international community. One way of representing the history of modern European thought is as a struggle between those who have wanted to claim everything for reason and those who, on the contrary, insist on the exclusive primacy of ultimately irrational psychological attributes as the foundation of a necessary and immutable identity. I have sought to show that this conception of identity is false, that our identity is grounded in language and that language itself has two modes of employment which I have distinguished as 'substantive' and 'formal'. But while I have argued that the possibility of political community is dependent on the development of the formal aspect of language, and that it can in this sense be regarded as superior, it does not follow that we can abandon the substantive, identity-forming, culturally specific aspect of language.

We cannot throw away our historically inherited language, our habitual modes of expression and understanding, because then we should be cast completely adrift, have no stable basis to begin to think from, indeed, be unable to think or act in any coherent fashion at all. Continuing to enlarge our understanding of the world and to grow in relationship with it presupposes that this growth is a never completed process and that we already have at least some understanding and some relationship, however partial or deficient.

Just as thought is a continuing and never ending exploration of the world which is funded at every stage by the generation of new questions and antinomies, or the regeneration of old questions in new guises, so the development of international community should be conceived not as a sudden transposition from benighted ignorance to a god-like understanding of everything and trouble-free relations with all. Completely easy relations are no relations. Indeed, absolutely rational relations are a contradiction in terms because the fulfilment of any relationship, if we think of it as dynamic, depends on the continuing mutual need of the partners – that is to say, on the persisting native partiality, deficiency and particularity of each. If the substantive aspect of our identity is not transformed and renewed in its particularity by our relationship with others, then the crucial contributary elements of the relationship will disappear, and with them will disappear also both the relationship and the original separate identities. Neither international community, nor the rational understanding which accompanies the formal use of language, should be imagined to dissolve identity. They can only arise out of identity and a given particular series of distinctive native attributes in the first place.

The function of reason is not to make us into perfect ghosts, or to displace or suffocate our particular psychological identity, but to train and reorient our unique but undeveloped and disarrayed natural proclivities into a disposition of harmony and balance, both amongst ourselves in our local world and in our relations with the wider world.[6] So our dependence on specific languages, with their own histories and inherited overall structure of meaning, is necessary to reason and should not, therefore, be misunderstood as an irrational obstacle to human progress. At the same time rationality and the development of active external relations should not be imagined to be inimical to cultural identity but on the contrary to be necessary to any thriving, open and developing culture.

It is not clear to what extent, if at all, the Kantian solution to the problem of international community envisages our leaving behind our specific cultural identity as something which, when we are rational, we will have grown out of and learnt to do without. If it does so then the account developed here is significantly different, because our specific cultural identity is here understood as the precondition of our continuing to make a positive contribution to an evolving rational community. With this qualification, however, Kant's central insight not only stands, but deserves to be repeated again and again. It is not just that, other things being equal, republics make for the most stable world (some have even alleged that this has been empirically disproved by modern events, though how it could be, since it is not an empirical point, is obscure) but that *pari passu* it is the type and quality of the *constitutions* in the international arena, whatever they are (not governments or peoples or policies) which condition the overall character and quality of the international relations within it. The triumph of empiricism in Western political thought is here an obstacle rather than an aid to understanding. We habitually overlook the importance of this point about quality because like fortune-tellers we are constantly looking for some rules of interpretation which will allow us to read what is in our tea-leaves straight off from socio-economic indices of one kind or another, from merely empirical series of attributes. But the whole point is that the type and quality of a constitution cannot be read off bare indices of any sort, and nor can the type and quality of the international system. The constitutional meaning of Gross National Product, or of the degree of physical integration between different national economies, cannot be discerned 'from the data' but only from knowing what effect these phenomena are having on the minds of the people in the countries concerned, and moreover what effect the minds of the people concerned are having on the different 'empirical' data.

The interpretation of constitutions is a question of meanings and judgement. A republic, like its converse, a tyranny, is defined formally – the one as a self-ruled public realm with a rational hold on its destiny, the other a realm from which the guiding hand of reason is absent and where destiny is in the hands of whim, fancy and blind fortune. Kant's contribution was to point out that if the world was composed of tyrannical and capricious constitutions, then it followed that the relations between them would also be capricious. They could not be anything else, even if there were honour amongst tyrannical thieves at the international level. From the point of view of a people deprived of exercising its own reason in the determination of its own life and destiny it makes little difference whether the tyrant comes to agreements with other tyrants over their heads or not. The constitutional position is the same either way – they have no say, by definition. Conversely, if it is the people in a particular realm who by thought and action control their own destiny in domestic affairs, who in other words do not so much inhabit a republic as *being* one, it will follow that they are in principle in control of their own deliberate foreign relations as well. There is a *logical* internal connection between the constitutional character of a state and the constitutional character of its external relations which makes it impossible for it to be in one constitutional condition internally whilst in another constitutional condition externally. Because there is a connection of logical entailment between the internal constitution and the constitutional character of its external behaviour, it also follows logically that a world of unreasonable domestic constitutions leads to a world of unreasonable international relations, and that a world of reasonable domestic constitutions would lead to a world of reasonable international relations, more or less, depending on the overall degree of enlightenment.

It is not my intention to claim that a world of harmonious relations is realisable, but only to indicate that rational foreign policy is a consequence of a rational constitution, so that foreign policy will be rational and just in proportion as and to the extent that the constitution of any state is rational and just, to the extent in other words that it *is* a republic.

This proposition leaves open the question of what a republic is, other than simply being a rationally self-ordered realm. I have given the germ of an answer to this question in the body of the chapter. The *sine qua non* of the existence of a republic in the traditional sense is not manhood suffrage but plurality of points of view. It is only a plurality of points of view which is capable of generating the basic conditions of public debate on questions of foreign policy. What makes for rational public debate on foreign policy is public interest, the availability of all the material facts, the education, the intelligence and the variety of native points of view of self-consciously public citizens, and a free press and media producing a genuine variety of informed opinion.

This may seem like a very tall order, though all the points I have just outlined ought to be perfectly unexceptionable. All it indicates is how short we fall from even beginning to approach a self-directed foreign policy in even the most 'advanced states', yet there really is no substitute for informed public debate on foreign policy if self-direction is what we really want. This is not to say that we need to be able to vote directly on every question of foreign policy in some attempt to imitate the Athenian assembly, but it means at the very least that the celebrated 'foreign policy maker' should be publicly accountable to an informed public opinion and not able to push anything past by resort either to secrecy or its near cousin the doctrine of special and privileged expertise.

I have said nothing about rules in the conception of international community I have outlined. This is simply because, except for certain implicit restraints which are in the spirit of rational foreign policy, the community has no explicit and detailed empirical structure. Just as it is up to the citizens of a republic how much of an institutional super-structure they wish to erect in order to serve their public purposes (in other words, it is up to them where exactly they wish to draw the line between public and private, since in a republic there is no independent sovereign arbiter), it is also up to them how much substantive business they wish to engage in internationally, and whether or not they wish to set up permanent institutions with independent executive powers in order to further their collective purposes. All this is simply a question of public judgement, at home as abroad, and therefore, with respect to its being pro- or anti-community, the question to ask about any international policy is not what it ostensibly does (reallocate resources, set up international organisations, or whatever) but what effect it has on the *public* communitarian relations between public realms.

As was noted in the Introduction to this book, the only specific duty towards individuals in Kant's world of republics was hospitality. The absence of rules is a simple consequence of the formality of the argument and should not be read necessarily to mark a distaste for substantive economic enterprises. The rule of hospitality is little more than an indication of the kind of attitude of mind which would accompany world public political relations. What it indicates above all else is a general disposition towards restraint in putting forward particular interests, and of forbearance towards the other, and this is precisely the general attitude we would deduce from the desire for a fruitful relationship between acknowledged opposites which we postulated earlier. But the whole purpose of this exercise, as I understand it, is not to stipulate the nuts and bolts of a working international system but to give an account of what a cosmopolitan political order would be constitutionally. In other words, it is not programmatic or instrumental, but it is still practical in that the argument produces a characteristic understanding of what it is to act in a cosmopolitan system, or rather consistently with that aim, namely, 'Be republican in foreign policy as at home, and therefore act with restraint and forbearance'. In fact, forbearance would seem to preclude on the whole engaging in any large-scale projects, but it would all depend on what republican constitutions would agree to severally and why. And that could not be predicted in advance of a particular case.

Neither my own formulation of the essence of international community, nor the Kantian one to which it is so similar, can produce automatic judgements on the international system as we find it; it is simply a question of going around case by case and saying, 'Was this policy or decision arrived at in a republican fashion, and with the restraint and forbearance which is consistent with a cosmopolitan outlook?' But even if this gives us no positive list of empirical checks with which to evaluate particular policies for their republican content (this is really only a matter of our own capacity to judge on the question of public responsibility), we can still gain a fairly shrewd idea of how far we have progressed on the road towards international community by asking ourselves how often it ever occurs to anybody to ask questions of this sort. It seems fairly obvious that the question is so unfamiliar to our current frame of mind as to be almost unintelligible. It is not necessarily the case that the outlook presented here is irrelevant on that account; the infrequency of the question may well be a guide to how far we still have to travel conceptually and the content of the question itself may well be a timely reminder.

NOTES: CHAPTER 12

1   The thinking behind this chapter has a number of sources, most prominent of which are the general revival in political philosophy which has come out of the revolution in linguistic philosophy of the 1950s and two works of Plato, the *Symposium* and the *Phaedrus*.

2   The most prominent recent claims that the major belief systems of the world boil down to a series of moral attitudes which could form the basis of a sense of world identity come from the various hands engaged on the 'World Order Models Project'.

3   J. B. Carroll (ed.), *Language, Thought and Reality: Selected Writings of Benjamin Lee Whorf* (Cambridge, Mass.: MIT Press, 1965).

4   See, for example, R. Rhees, 'Can there be a private language?', in G. Pitcher (ed.), *Wittgenstein* (London: Macmillan, 1968), pp. 267–85.

5   The most familiar examples are the Greeks, Ancient Israel and China, but there are many cultures where the world as a whole is explained in terms of a cosmology which includes very localised features of the landscape.

6   The most concise modern formulation of the Platonic conception of thought which is represented here is Gottlob Frege, 'The thought: a logical enquiry', reprinted in P. F. Strawson (ed.), *Philosophical Logic* (London: Oxford University Press, 1967), pp. 7–38.

Index

MAYALL, ed. The Community of States

copy